THE OR...

THE

FORGE™

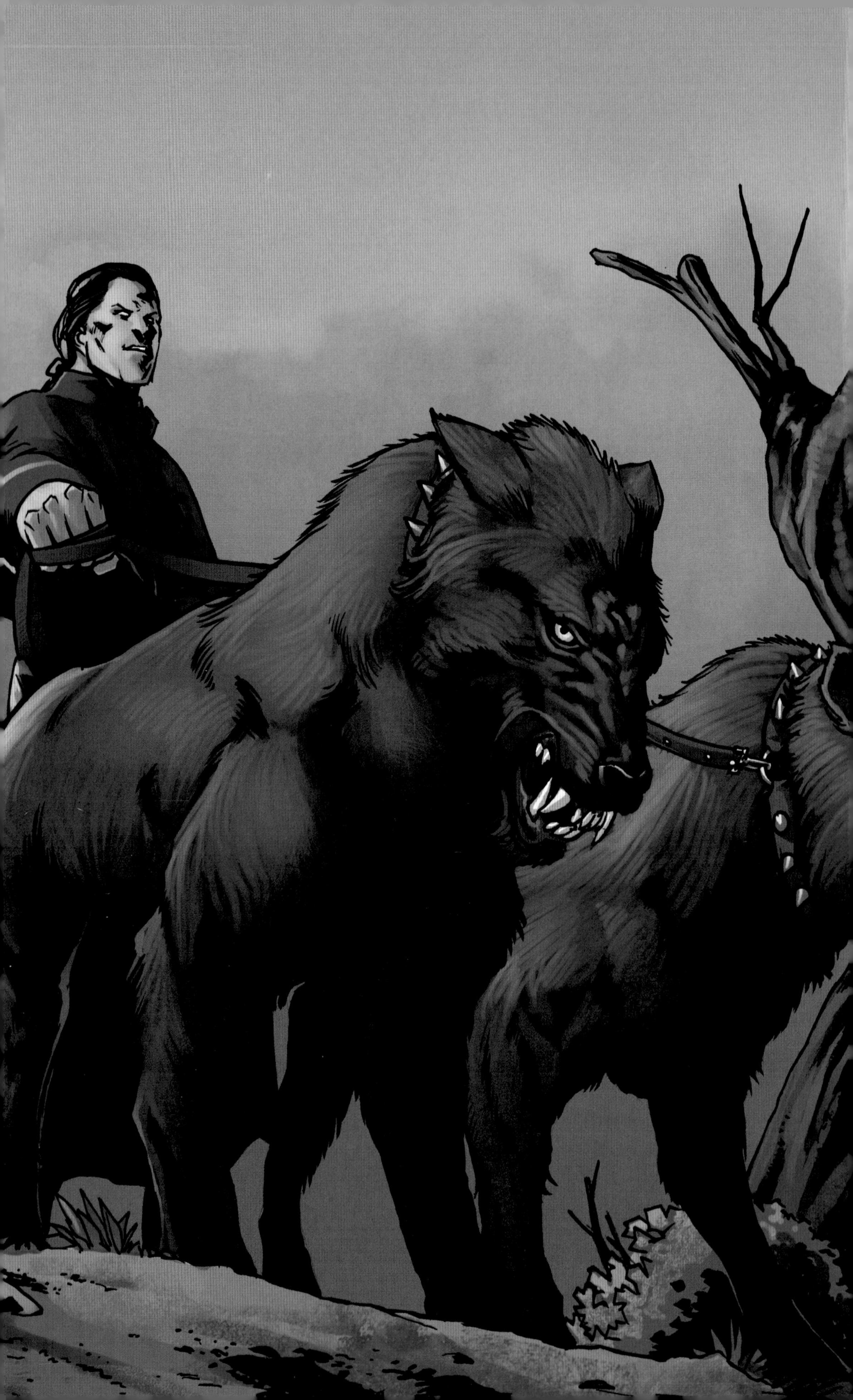

THE ORDER OF
THE
FORGE™

—CREATED BY DONN D. BERDAHL—

SCRIPT
VICTOR GISCHLER

ART
TAZIO BETTIN

COLORING ASSISTANCE
ENRICA EREN ANGIOLINI

LETTERING
NATE PIEKOS OF BLAMBOT ®

COVER AND CHAPTER BREAK ART
JUAN FERREYRA

ORIGINAL CHARACTER DESIGN
ERNESTO OCHOA

COMIC DEVELOPED BY
DONN D. BERDAHL & BILL SCHULTZ

ORIGINAL STORY BY
DONN D. BERDAHL & ANDY BRIGGS

DARK HORSE BOOKS

PRESIDENT AND PUBLISHER
MIKE RICHARDSON

EDITOR
DANIEL CHABON

ASSISTANT EDITOR
IAN TUCKER

DESIGNER
ETHAN KIMBERLING

DIGITAL ART TECHNICIAN
RYAN JORGENSEN

SPECIAL THANKS TO LAURA FORST AND EVIE YANNAKIDIS

NEIL HANKERSON, EXECUTIVE VICE PRESIDENT | TOM WEDDLE, CHIEF FINANCIAL OFFICER | RANDY STRADLEY, VICE PRESIDENT OF PUBLISHING | MICHAEL MARTENS, VICE PRESIDENT OF BOOK TRADE SALES SCOTT ALLIE, EDITOR IN CHIEF | MATT PARKINSON, VICE PRESIDENT OF MARKETING | DAVID SCROGGY, VICE PRESIDENT OF PRODUCT DEVELOPMENT | DALE LaFOUNTAIN, VICE PRESIDENT OF INFORMATION TECHNOLOGY | DARLENE VOGEL, SENIOR DIRECTOR OF PRINT, DESIGN, AND PRODUCTION | KEN LIZZI, GENERAL COUNSEL | DAVEY ESTRADA, EDITORIAL DIRECTOR | CHRIS WARNER, SENIOR BOOKS EDITOR CARY GRAZZINI, DIRECTOR OF PRINT AND DEVELOPMENT | LIA RIBACCHI, ART DIRECTOR | CARA NIECE, DIRECTOR OF SCHEDULING | MARK BERNARDI, DIRECTOR OF DIGITAL PUBLISHING

PUBLISHED BY DARK HORSE BOOKS
A DIVISION OF DARK HORSE COMICS, INC.
10956 SE MAIN STREET
MILWAUKIE, OR 97222

FIRST EDITION: NOVEMBER 2015
ISBN 978-1-61655-829-1

10 9 8 7 6 5 4 3 2 1
PRINTED IN CHINA

INTERNATIONAL LICENSING: (503) 905-2377
COMIC SHOP LOCATOR SERVICE: (888) 266-4226

THIS VOLUME COLLECTS *THE ORDER OF THE FORGE* #1–#3.

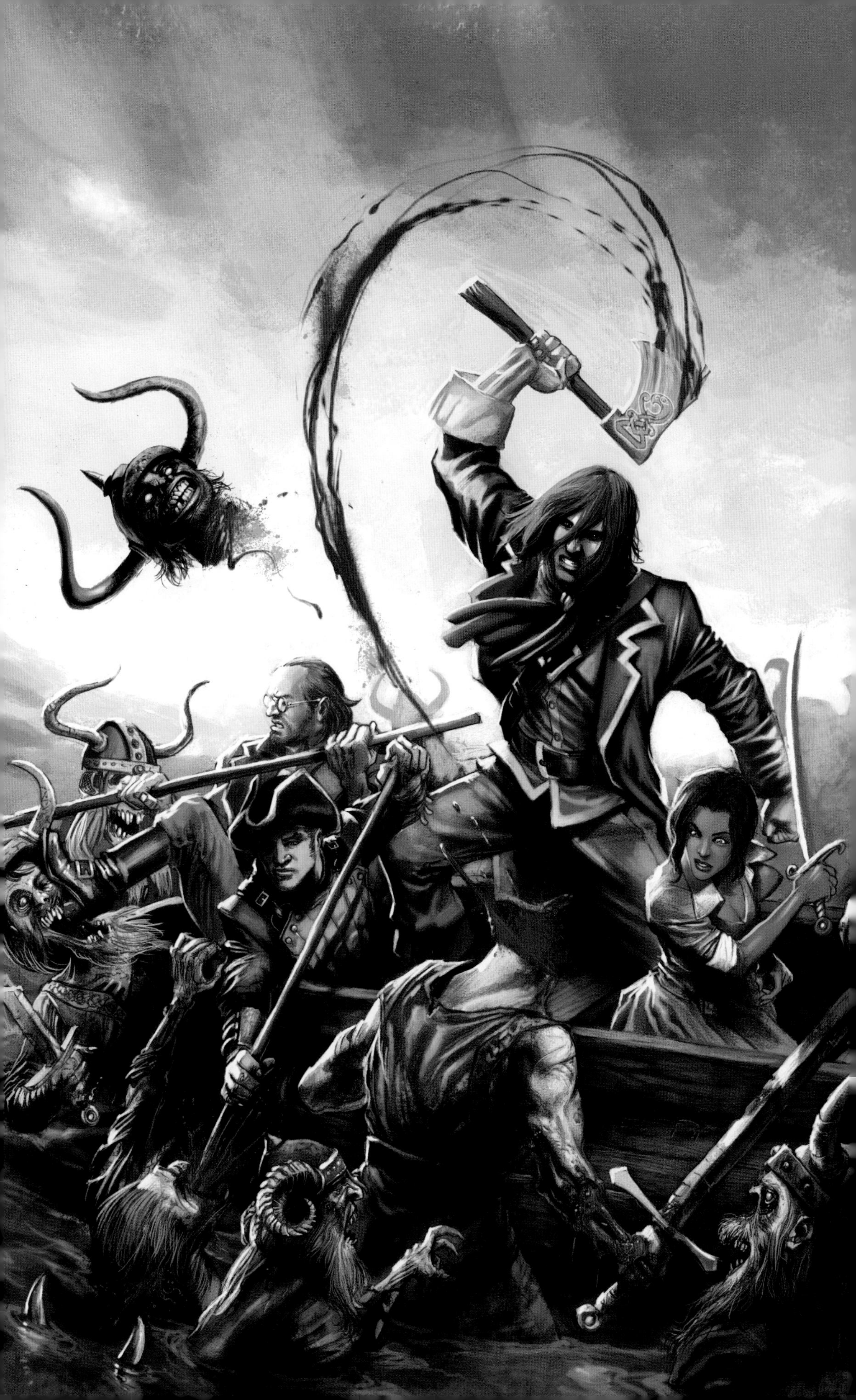

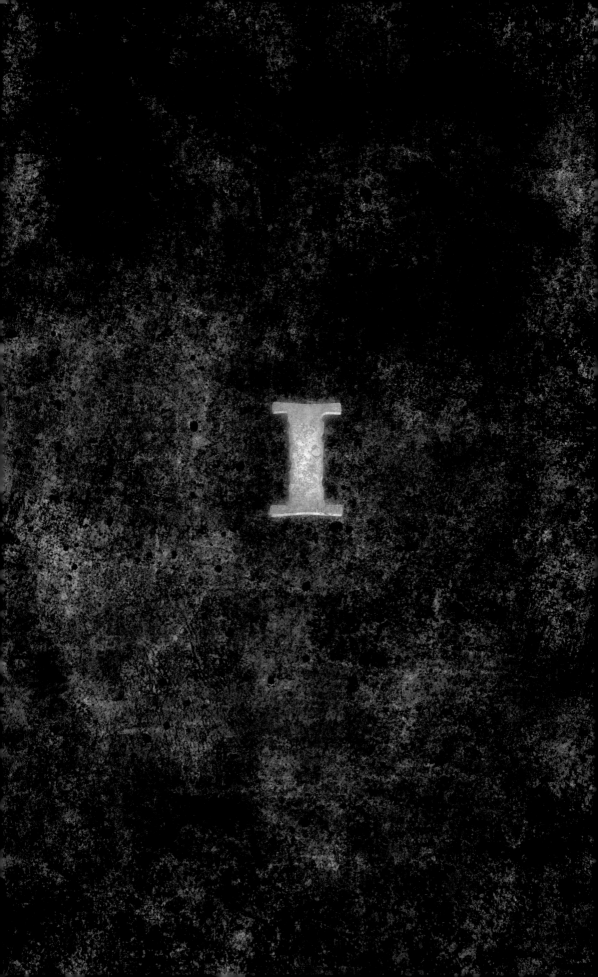

I

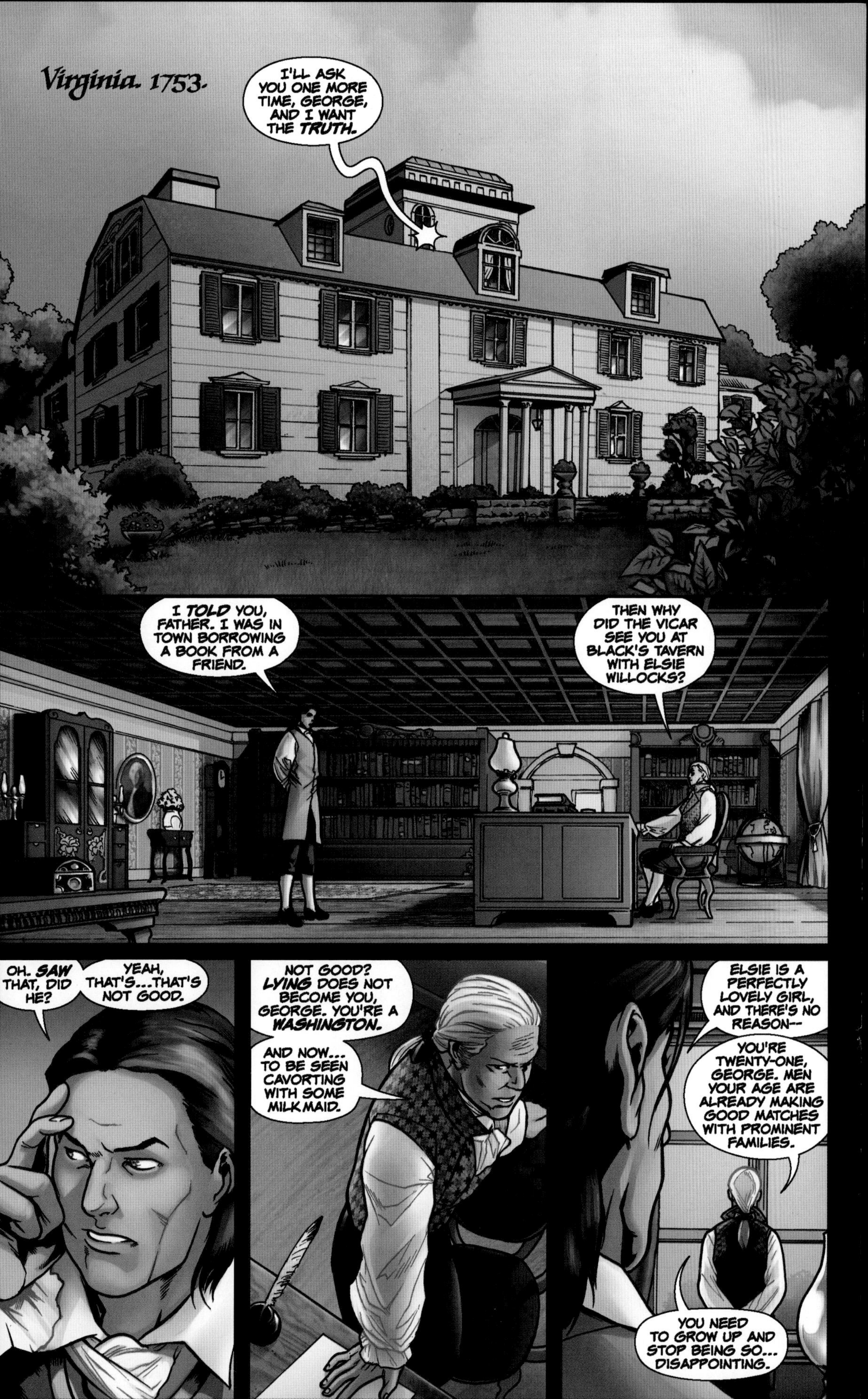
Virginia. 1753.
I'LL ASK YOU ONE MORE TIME, GEORGE, AND I WANT THE TRUTH.
I TOLD YOU, FATHER. I WAS IN TOWN BORROWING A BOOK FROM A FRIEND.
THEN WHY DID THE VICAR SEE YOU AT BLACK'S TAVERN WITH ELSIE WILLOCKS?
OH. SAW THAT, DID HE?
YEAH, THAT'S...THAT'S NOT GOOD.
NOT GOOD? LYING DOES NOT BECOME YOU, GEORGE. YOU'RE A WASHINGTON.
AND NOW... TO BE SEEN CAVORTING WITH SOME MILKMAID.
ELSIE IS A PERFECTLY LOVELY GIRL, AND THERE'S NO REASON--
YOU'RE TWENTY-ONE, GEORGE. MEN YOUR AGE ARE ALREADY MAKING GOOD MATCHES WITH PROMINENT FAMILIES.
YOU NEED TO GROW UP AND STOP BEING SO... DISAPPOINTING.

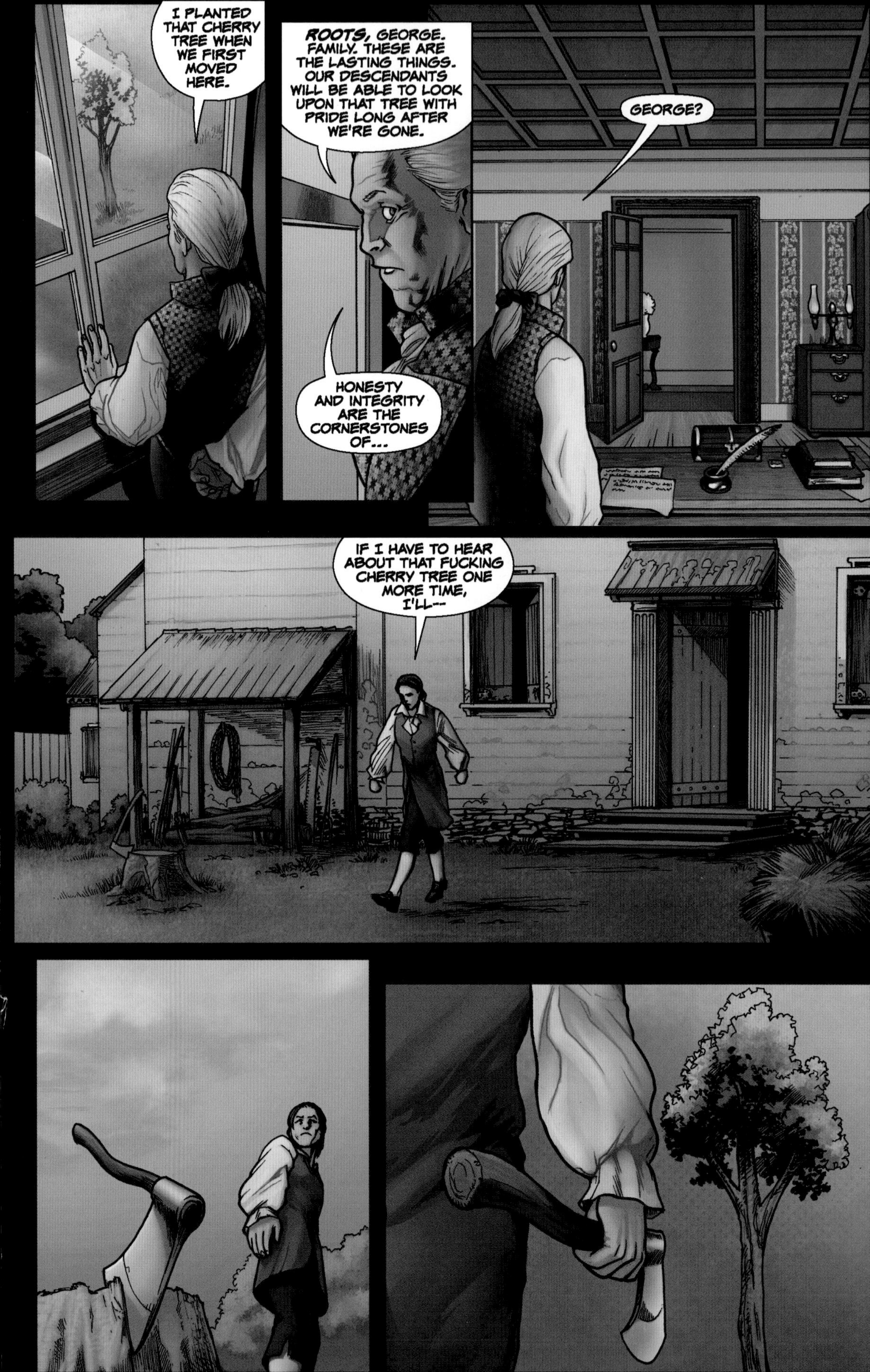
I PLANTED THAT CHERRY TREE WHEN WE FIRST MOVED HERE.
ROOTS, GEORGE. FAMILY. THESE ARE THE LASTING THINGS. OUR DESCENDANTS WILL BE ABLE TO LOOK UPON THAT TREE WITH PRIDE LONG AFTER WE'RE GONE.
HONESTY AND INTEGRITY ARE THE CORNERSTONES OF...
GEORGE?
IF I HAVE TO HEAR ABOUT THAT FUCKING CHERRY TREE ONE MORE TIME, I'LL--

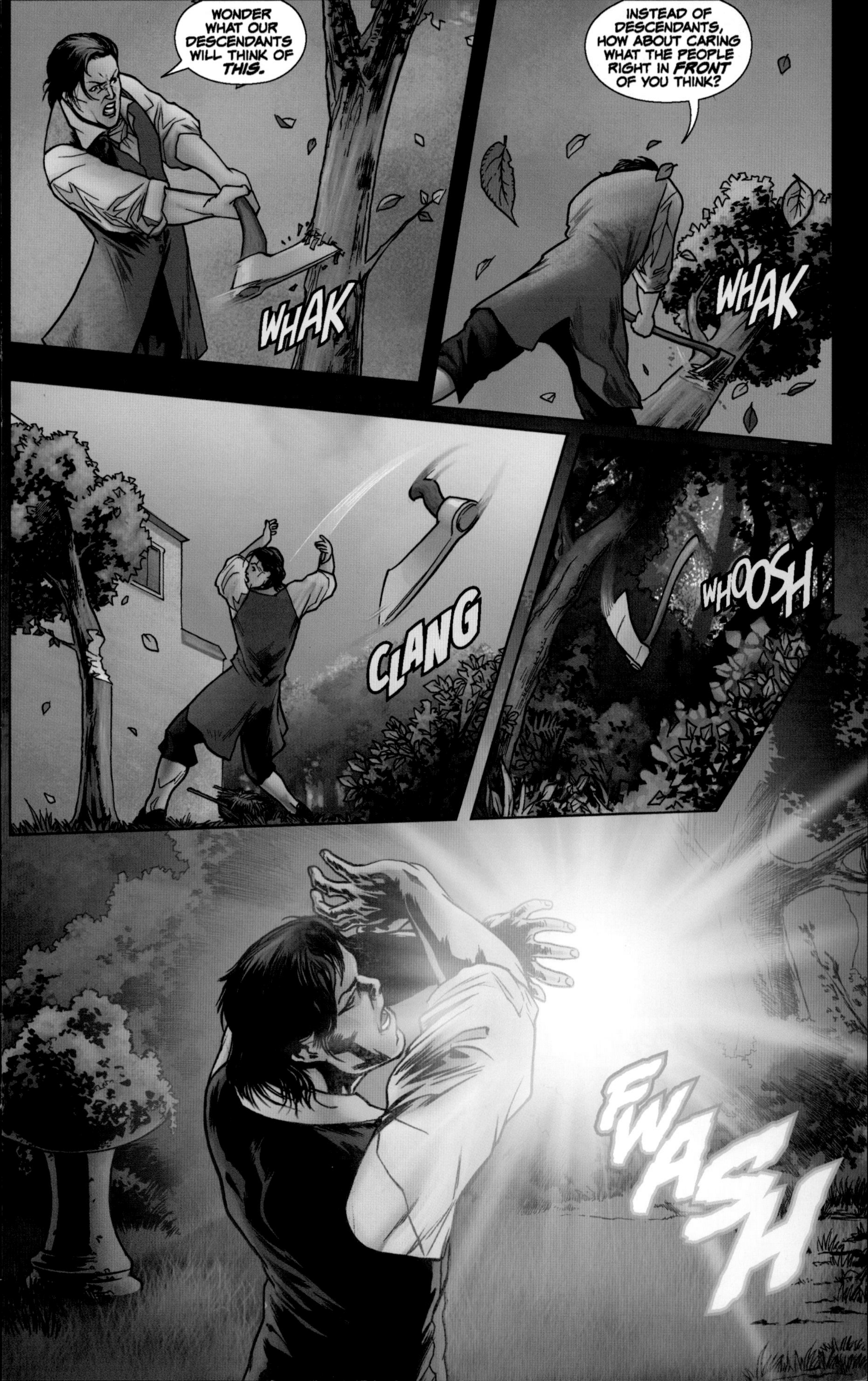
WONDER WHAT OUR DESCENDANTS WILL THINK OF THIS.
WHAK
INSTEAD OF DESCENDANTS, HOW ABOUT CARING WHAT THE PEOPLE RIGHT IN FRONT OF YOU THINK?
WHAK
CLANG
WHOOSH
FWASH

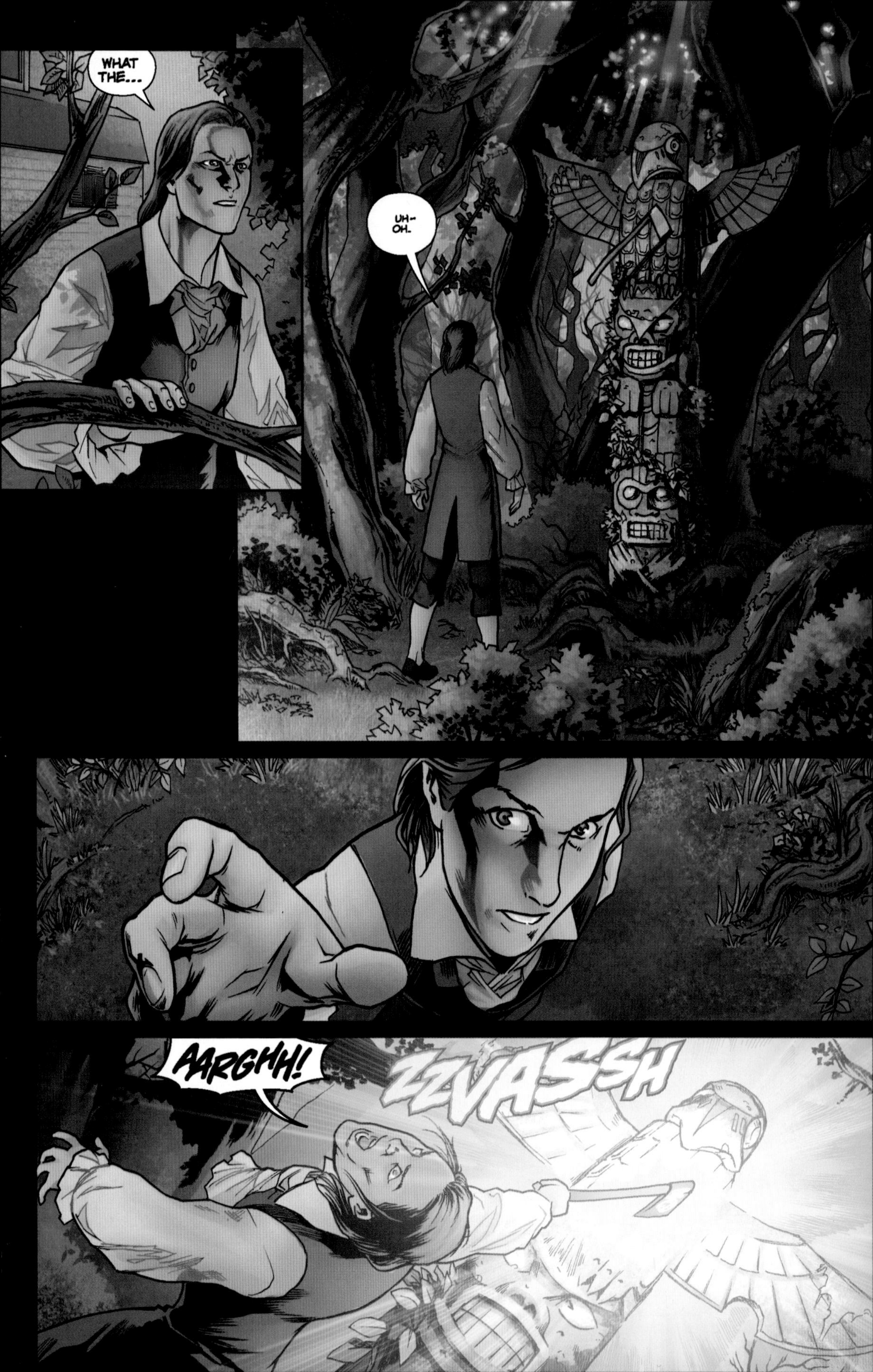
WHAT THE...
UH-OH.
AARGHH!
ZZVASSH

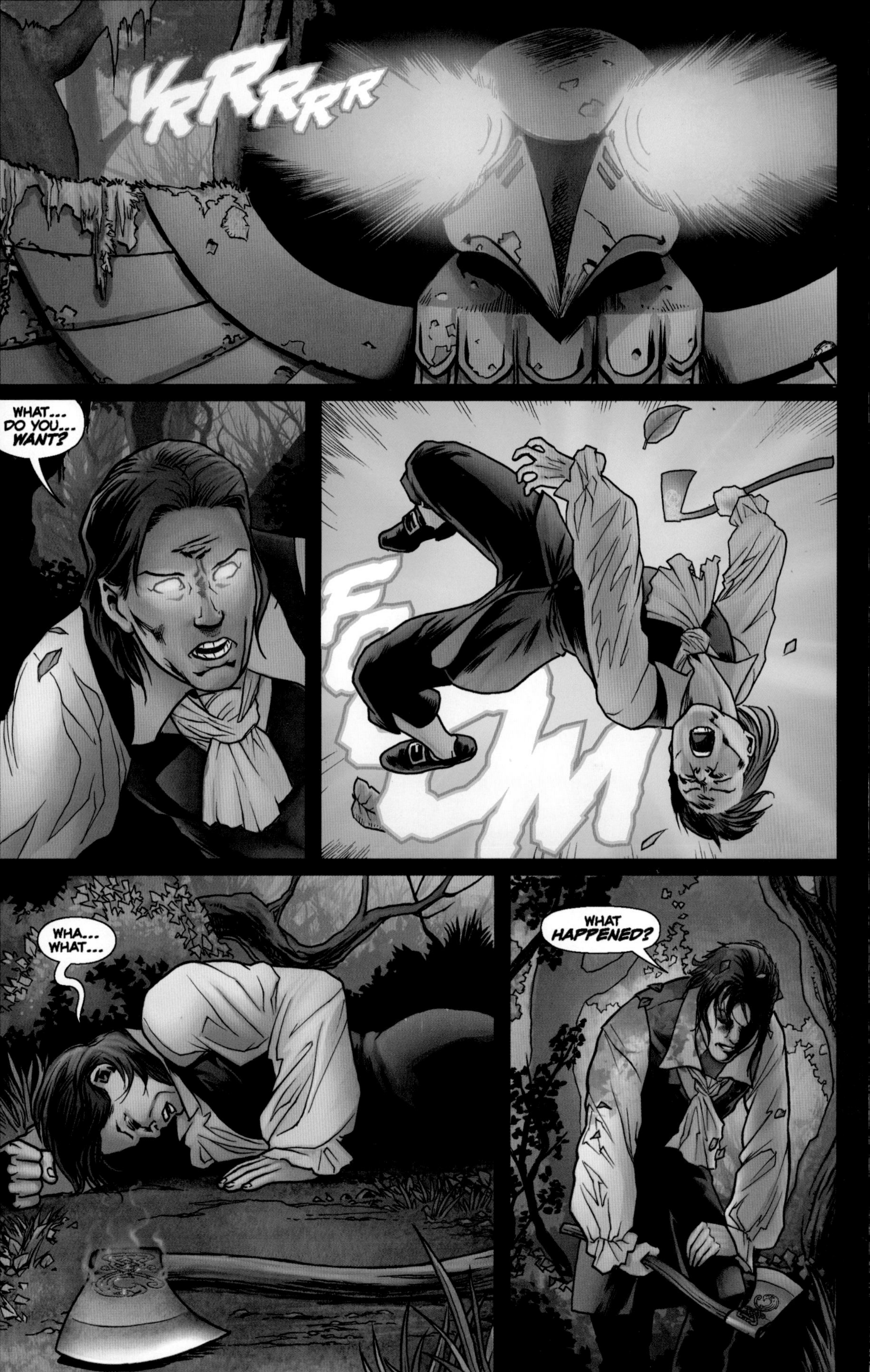
VRRRRRR
WHAT... DO YOU... WANT?
FOOM
WHA... WHAT...
WHAT HAPPENED?

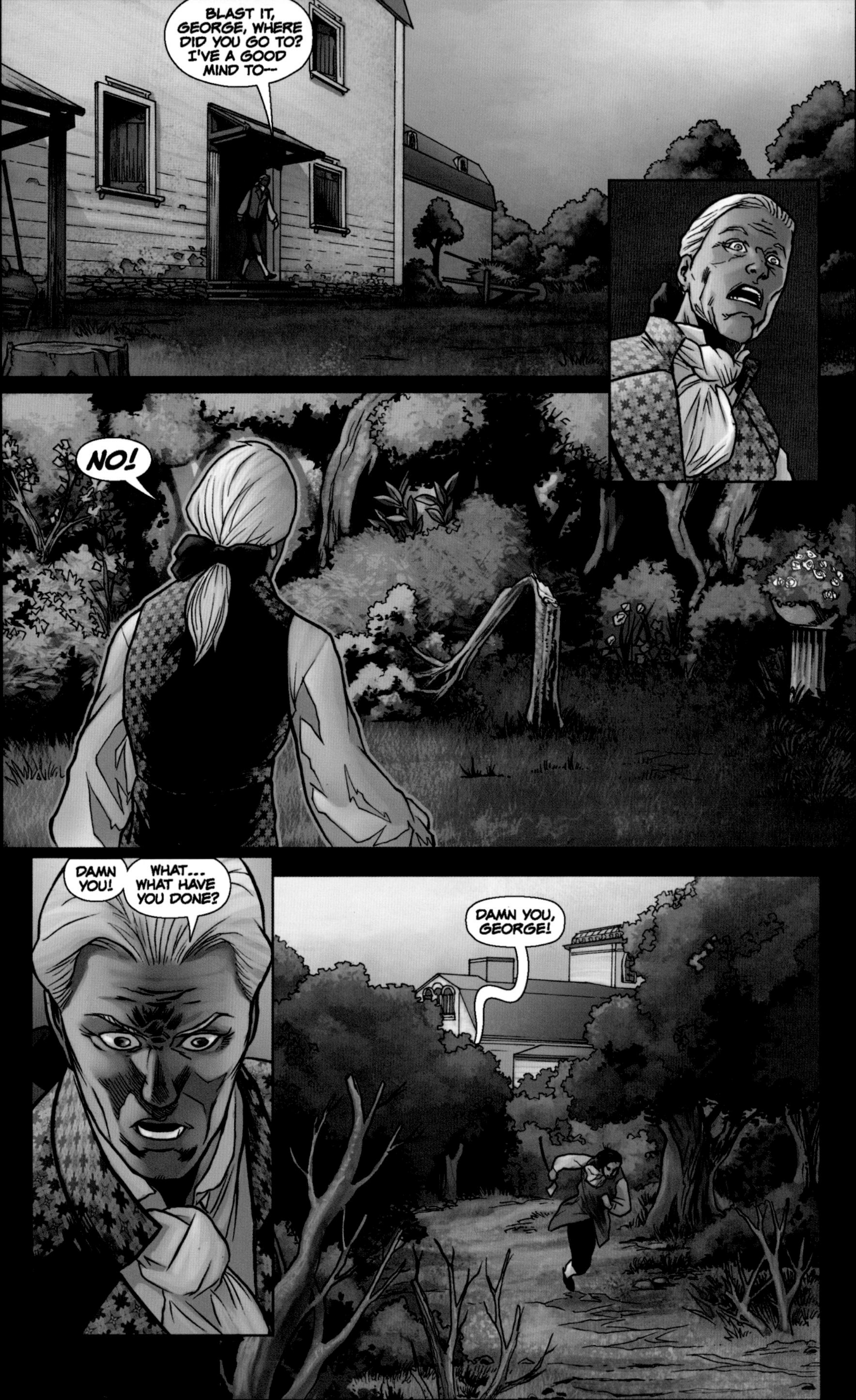
BLAST IT, GEORGE, WHERE DID YOU GO TO? I'VE A GOOD MIND TO--
NO!
DAMN YOU!
WHAT... WHAT HAVE YOU DONE?
DAMN YOU, GEORGE!

Six months later...

Philadelphia.

DEAR FATHER, I AM MOST SINCERELY *SORRY* THAT...

WELL...NO, THAT'S NOT *QUITE* TRUE, IS IT?

SO...AN APOLOGY.

BUT AN *HONEST* ONE.

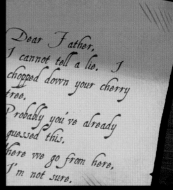

Dear Father,
I cannot tell a lie. I
chopped down your cherry
tree.
Probably you've already
guessed this.
Where we go from here,
I'm not sure.

STILL WORKING ON THAT LETTER?

IT'S NOT SO SIMPLE.

A FEW LITTLE WHITE LIES ABOUT HOW REGRETFUL YOU ARE. SIMPLE.

TRUST ME. *NOT SO* SIMPLE.

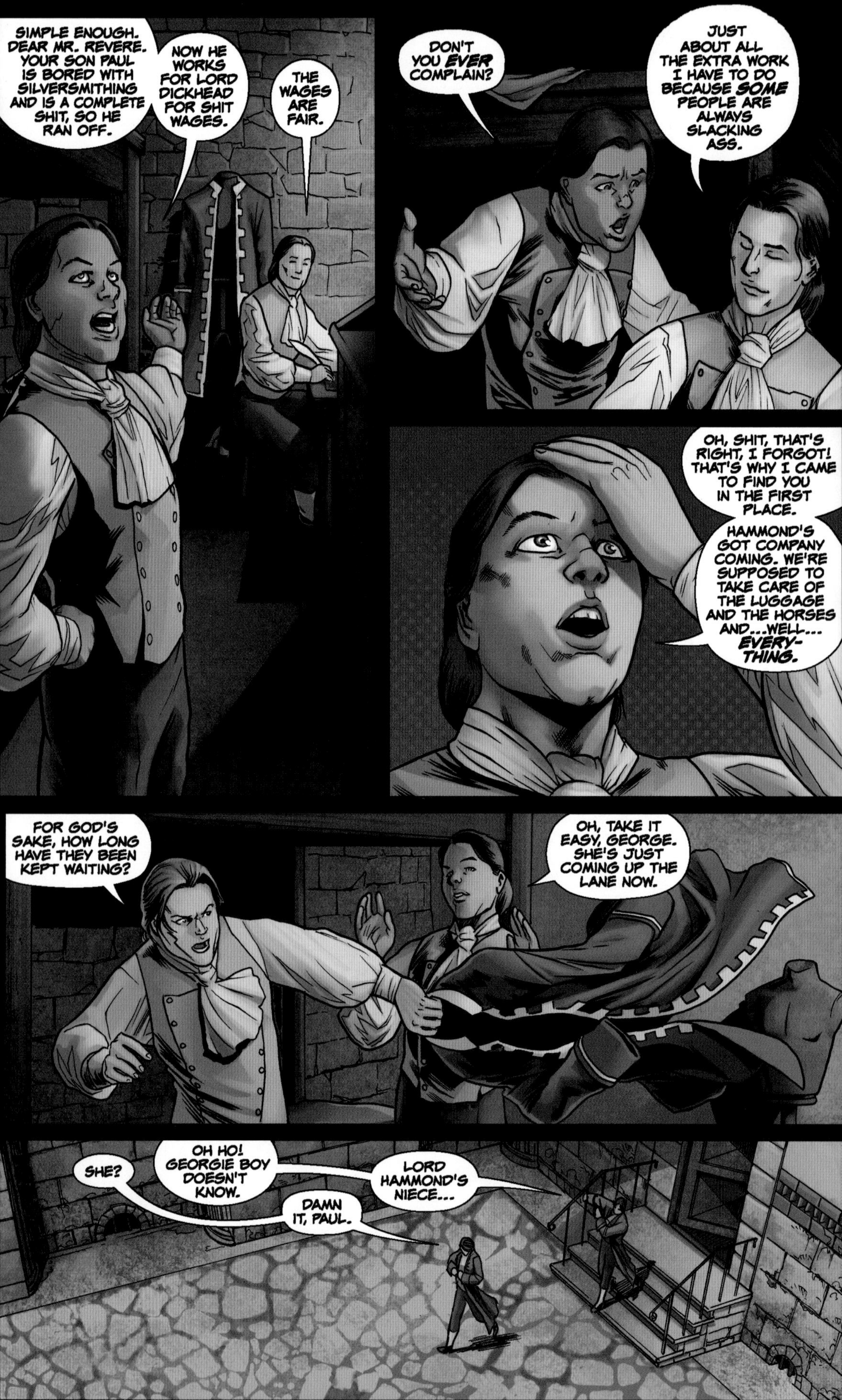
SIMPLE ENOUGH. DEAR MR. REVERE. YOUR SON PAUL IS BORED WITH SILVERSMITHING AND IS A COMPLETE SHIT, SO HE RAN OFF.
NOW HE WORKS FOR LORD DICKHEAD FOR SHIT WAGES.
THE WAGES ARE FAIR.
DON'T YOU EVER COMPLAIN?
JUST ABOUT ALL THE EXTRA WORK I HAVE TO DO BECAUSE SOME PEOPLE ARE ALWAYS SLACKING ASS.
OH, SHIT, THAT'S RIGHT, I FORGOT! THAT'S WHY I CAME TO FIND YOU IN THE FIRST PLACE.
HAMMOND'S GOT COMPANY COMING. WE'RE SUPPOSED TO TAKE CARE OF THE LUGGAGE AND THE HORSES AND...WELL... EVERY-THING.
FOR GOD'S SAKE, HOW LONG HAVE THEY BEEN KEPT WAITING?
OH, TAKE IT EASY, GEORGE. SHE'S JUST COMING UP THE LANE NOW.
SHE?
OH HO! GEORGIE BOY DOESN'T KNOW.
LORD HAMMOND'S NIECE...
DAMN IT, PAUL.

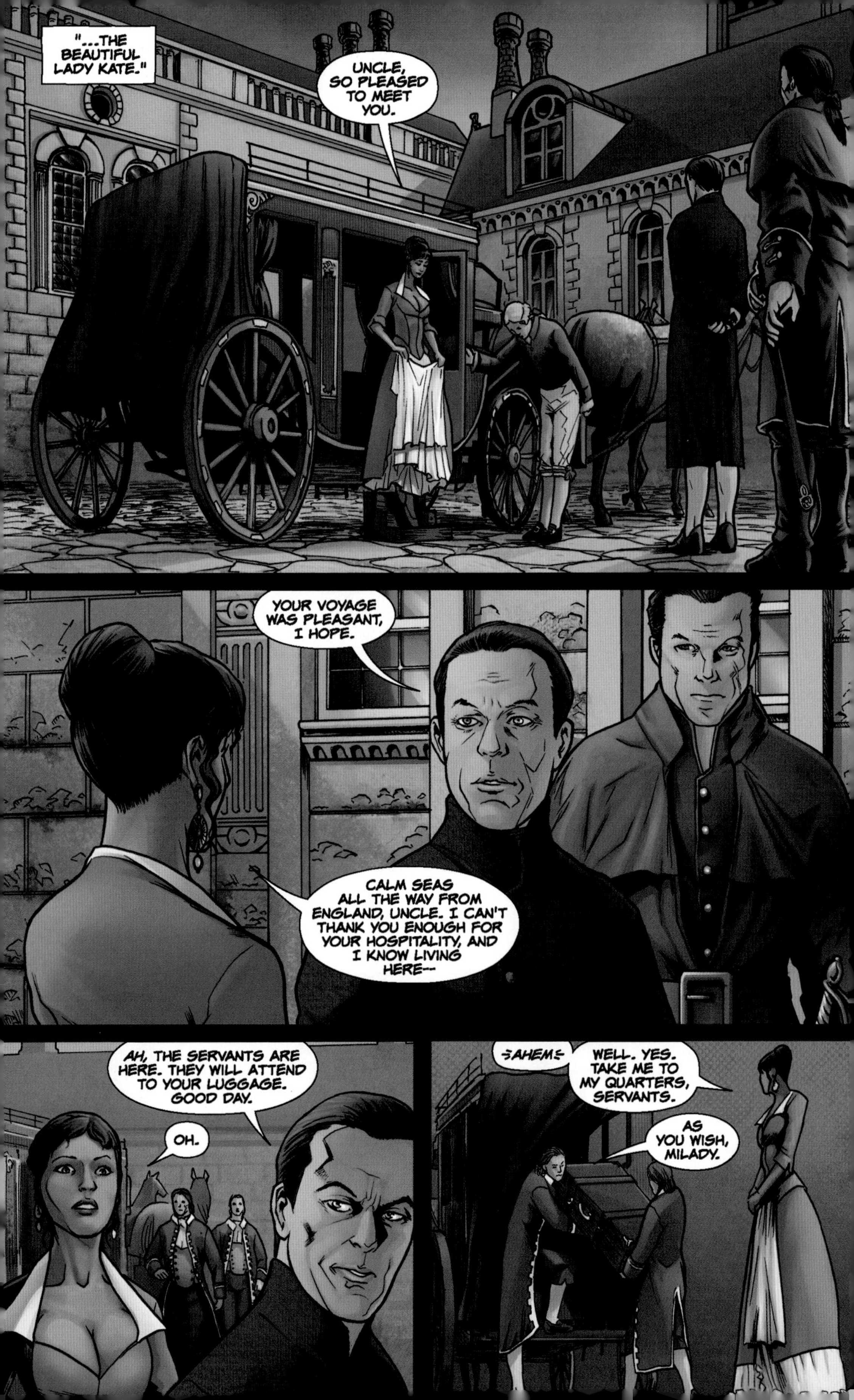
"...THE BEAUTIFUL LADY KATE."
UNCLE, SO PLEASED TO MEET YOU.
YOUR VOYAGE WAS PLEASANT, I HOPE.
CALM SEAS ALL THE WAY FROM ENGLAND, UNCLE. I CAN'T THANK YOU ENOUGH FOR YOUR HOSPITALITY, AND I KNOW LIVING HERE--
AH, THE SERVANTS ARE HERE. THEY WILL ATTEND TO YOUR LUGGAGE. GOOD DAY.
OH.
=AHEM=
WELL. YES. TAKE ME TO MY QUARTERS, SERVANTS.
AS YOU WISH, MILADY.

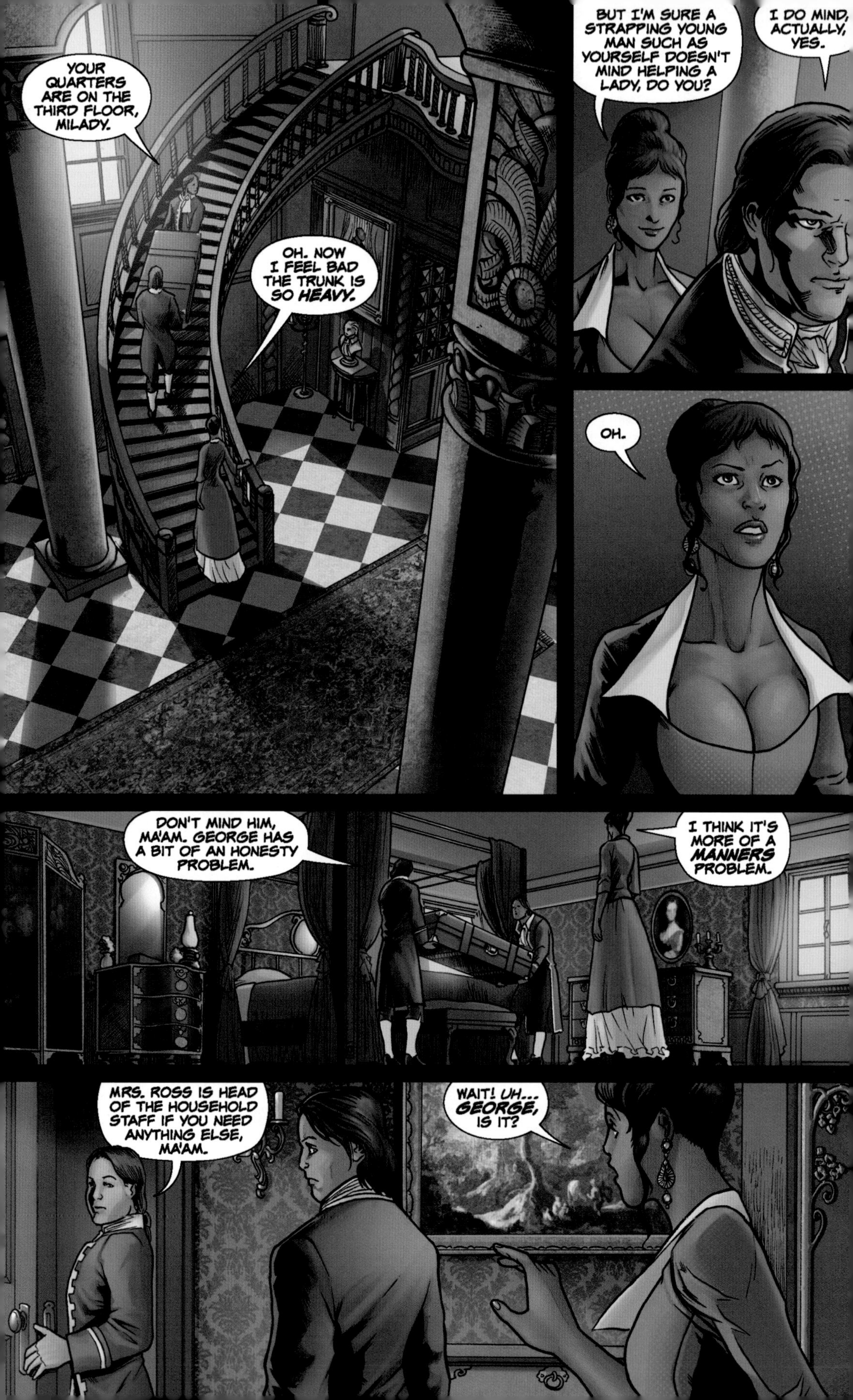
YOUR QUARTERS ARE ON THE THIRD FLOOR, MILADY.
OH. NOW I FEEL BAD THE TRUNK IS SO *HEAVY.*
BUT I'M SURE A STRAPPING YOUNG MAN SUCH AS YOURSELF DOESN'T MIND HELPING A LADY, DO YOU?
I DO MIND, ACTUALLY, YES.
OH.
DON'T MIND HIM, MA'AM. GEORGE HAS A BIT OF AN HONESTY PROBLEM.
I THINK IT'S MORE OF A *MANNERS* PROBLEM.
MRS. ROSS IS HEAD OF THE HOUSEHOLD STAFF IF YOU NEED ANYTHING ELSE, MA'AM.
WAIT! *UH... GEORGE,* IS IT?

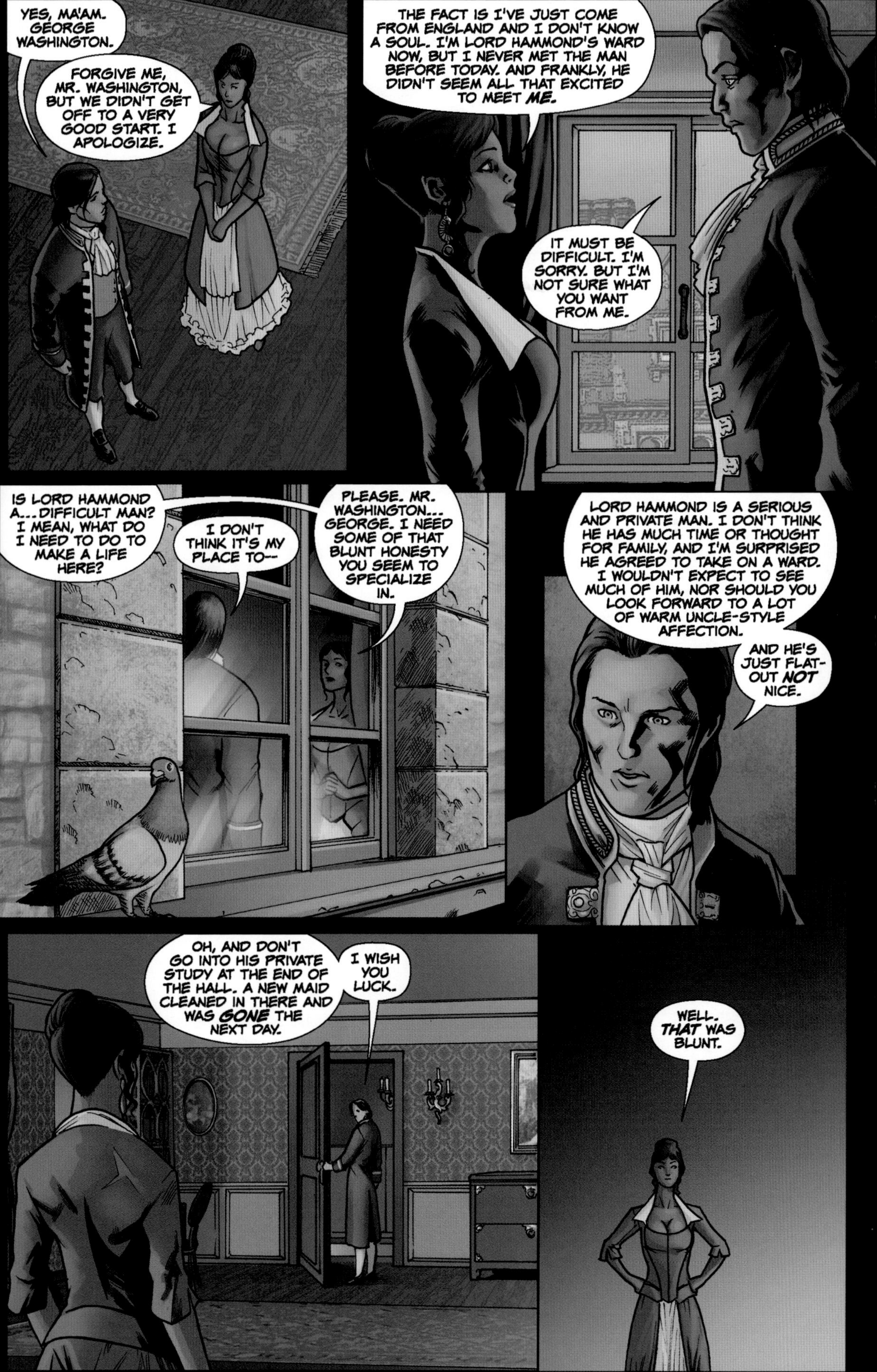
YES, MA'AM. GEORGE WASHINGTON.
FORGIVE ME, MR. WASHINGTON, BUT WE DIDN'T GET OFF TO A VERY GOOD START. I APOLOGIZE.
THE FACT IS I'VE JUST COME FROM ENGLAND AND I DON'T KNOW A SOUL. I'M LORD HAMMOND'S WARD NOW, BUT I NEVER MET THE MAN BEFORE TODAY. AND FRANKLY, HE DIDN'T SEEM ALL THAT EXCITED TO MEET *ME.*
IT MUST BE DIFFICULT. I'M SORRY. BUT I'M NOT SURE WHAT YOU WANT FROM ME.
IS LORD HAMMOND A... DIFFICULT MAN? I MEAN, WHAT DO I NEED TO DO TO MAKE A LIFE HERE?
I DON'T THINK IT'S MY PLACE TO--
PLEASE. MR. WASHINGTON... GEORGE. I NEED SOME OF THAT BLUNT HONESTY YOU SEEM TO SPECIALIZE IN.
LORD HAMMOND IS A SERIOUS AND PRIVATE MAN. I DON'T THINK HE HAS MUCH TIME OR THOUGHT FOR FAMILY, AND I'M SURPRISED HE AGREED TO TAKE ON A WARD. I WOULDN'T EXPECT TO SEE MUCH OF HIM, NOR SHOULD YOU LOOK FORWARD TO A LOT OF WARM UNCLE-STYLE AFFECTION.
AND HE'S JUST FLAT-OUT *NOT* NICE.
OH, AND DON'T GO INTO HIS PRIVATE STUDY AT THE END OF THE HALL. A NEW MAID CLEANED IN THERE AND WAS *GONE* THE NEXT DAY.
I WISH YOU LUCK.
WELL. *THAT* WAS BLUNT.

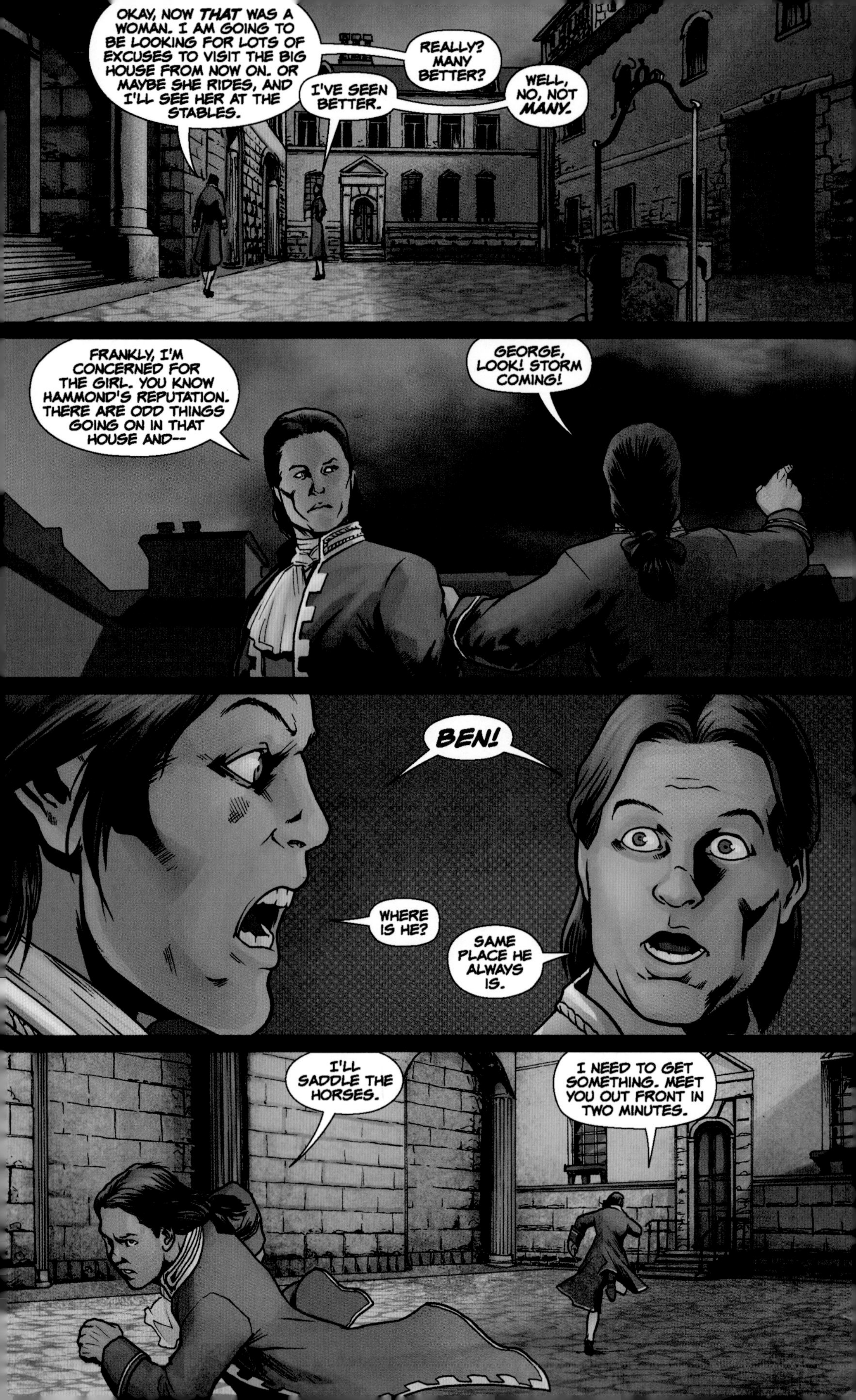
OKAY, NOW THAT WAS A WOMAN. I AM GOING TO BE LOOKING FOR LOTS OF EXCUSES TO VISIT THE BIG HOUSE FROM NOW ON. OR MAYBE SHE RIDES, AND I'LL SEE HER AT THE STABLES.
I'VE SEEN BETTER.
REALLY? MANY BETTER?
WELL, NO, NOT MANY.
FRANKLY, I'M CONCERNED FOR THE GIRL. YOU KNOW HAMMOND'S REPUTATION. THERE ARE ODD THINGS GOING ON IN THAT HOUSE AND--
GEORGE, LOOK! STORM COMING!
BEN!
WHERE IS HE?
SAME PLACE HE ALWAYS IS.
I'LL SADDLE THE HORSES.
I NEED TO GET SOMETHING. MEET YOU OUT FRONT IN TWO MINUTES.

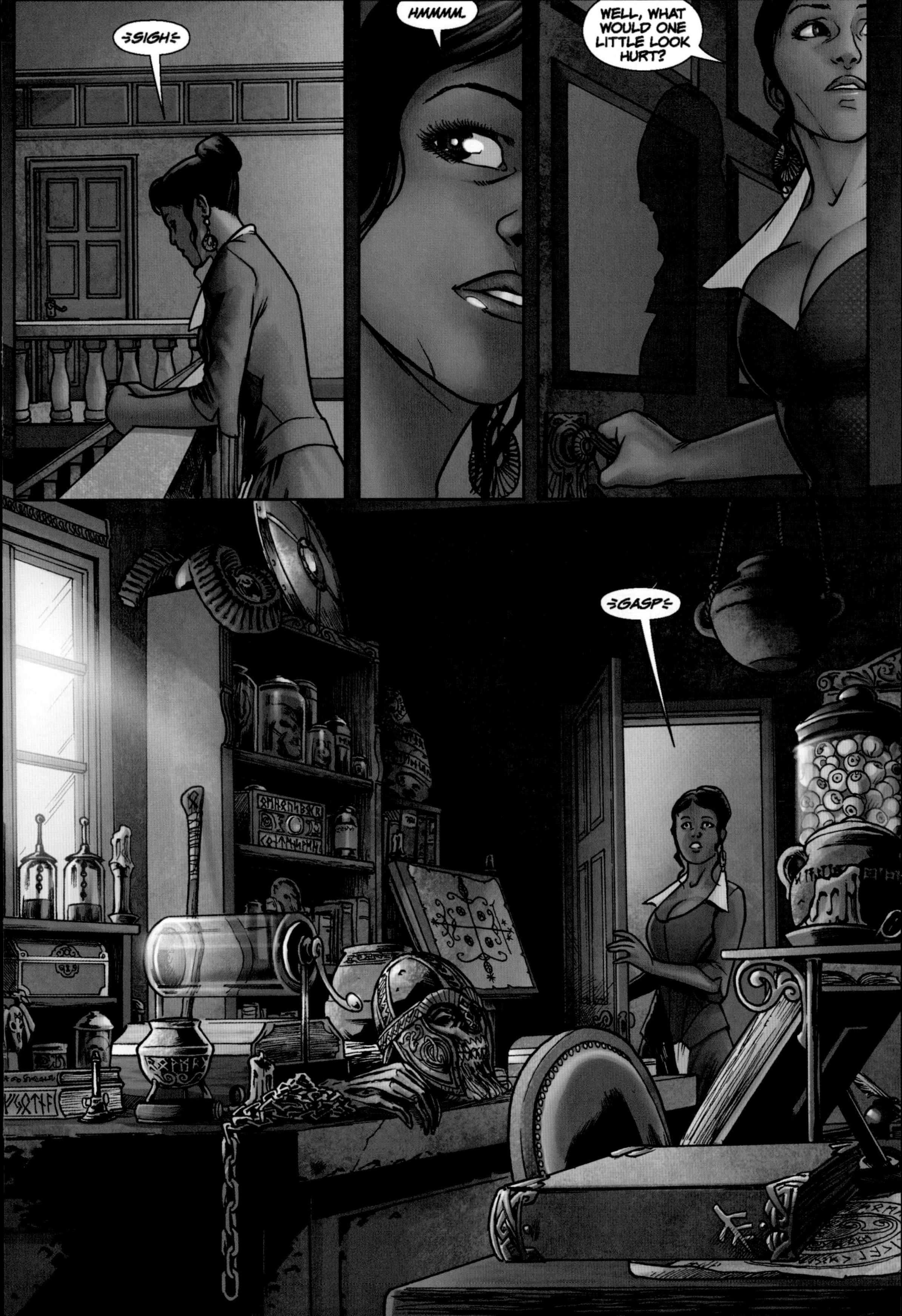

SIGH
HMMMM.
WELL, WHAT WOULD ONE LITTLE LOOK HURT?
GASP

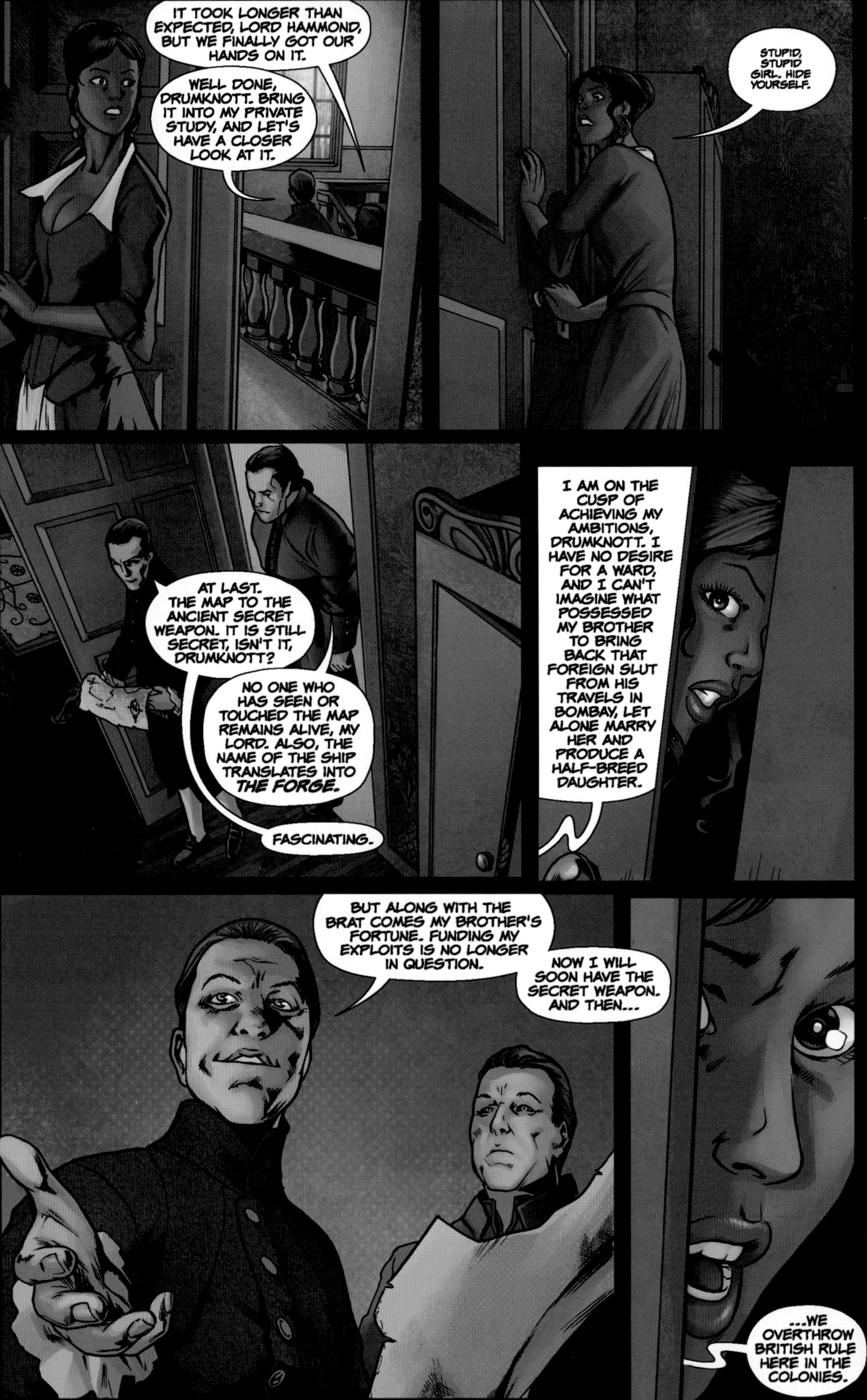
IT TOOK LONGER THAN EXPECTED, LORD HAMMOND, BUT WE FINALLY GOT OUR HANDS ON IT.
WELL DONE, DRUMKNOTT. BRING IT INTO MY PRIVATE STUDY, AND LET'S HAVE A CLOSER LOOK AT IT.
STUPID, STUPID GIRL. HIDE YOURSELF.
AT LAST. THE MAP TO THE ANCIENT SECRET WEAPON. IT IS STILL SECRET, ISN'T IT, DRUMKNOTT?
NO ONE WHO HAS SEEN OR TOUCHED THE MAP REMAINS ALIVE, MY LORD. ALSO, THE NAME OF THE SHIP TRANSLATES INTO *THE FORGE*.
FASCINATING.
I AM ON THE CUSP OF ACHIEVING MY AMBITIONS, DRUMKNOTT. I HAVE NO DESIRE FOR A WARD, AND I CAN'T IMAGINE WHAT POSSESSED MY BROTHER TO BRING BACK THAT FOREIGN SLUT FROM HIS TRAVELS IN BOMBAY, LET ALONE MARRY HER AND PRODUCE A HALF-BREED DAUGHTER.
BUT ALONG WITH THE BRAT COMES MY BROTHER'S FORTUNE. FUNDING MY EXPLOITS IS NO LONGER IN QUESTION.
NOW I WILL SOON HAVE THE SECRET WEAPON. AND THEN...
...WE OVERTHROW BRITISH RULE HERE IN THE COLONIES.

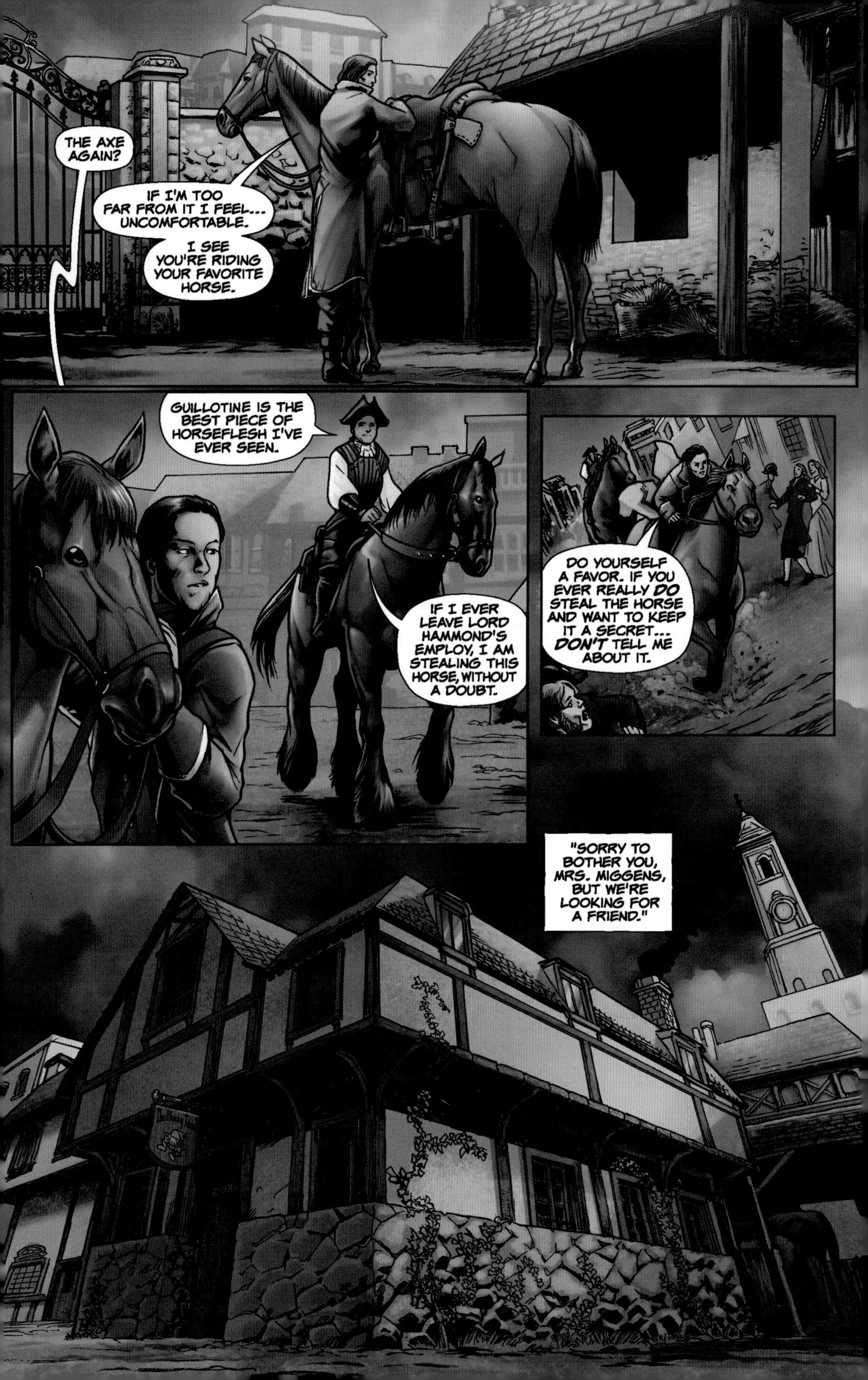
THE AXE AGAIN?
IF I'M TOO FAR FROM IT I FEEL... UNCOMFORTABLE.
I SEE YOU'RE RIDING YOUR FAVORITE HORSE.
GUILLOTINE IS THE BEST PIECE OF HORSEFLESH I'VE EVER SEEN.
IF I EVER LEAVE LORD HAMMOND'S EMPLOY, I AM STEALING THIS HORSE, WITHOUT A DOUBT.
DO YOURSELF A FAVOR. IF YOU EVER REALLY *DO* STEAL THE HORSE AND WANT TO KEEP IT A SECRET... *DON'T* TELL ME ABOUT IT.
"SORRY TO BOTHER YOU, MRS. MIGGENS, BUT WE'RE LOOKING FOR A FRIEND."

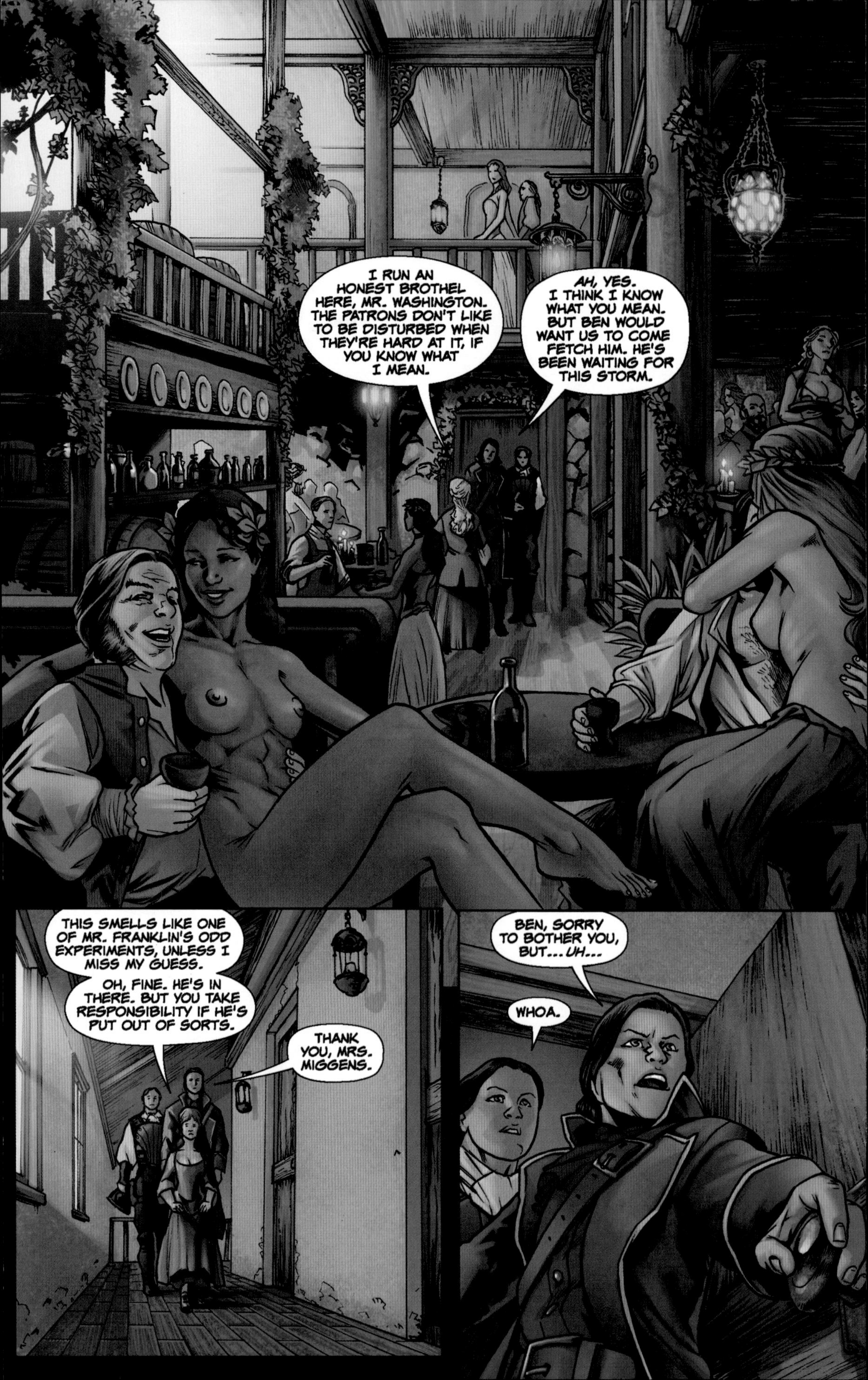
I RUN AN HONEST BROTHEL HERE, MR. WASHINGTON. THE PATRONS DON'T LIKE TO BE DISTURBED WHEN THEY'RE HARD AT IT, IF YOU KNOW WHAT I MEAN.
AH, YES. I THINK I KNOW WHAT YOU MEAN. BUT BEN WOULD WANT US TO COME FETCH HIM. HE'S BEEN WAITING FOR THIS STORM.
THIS SMELLS LIKE ONE OF MR. FRANKLIN'S ODD EXPERIMENTS, UNLESS I MISS MY GUESS.
OH, FINE. HE'S IN THERE. BUT YOU TAKE RESPONSIBILITY IF HE'S PUT OUT OF SORTS.
THANK YOU, MRS. MIGGENS.
BEN, SORRY TO BOTHER YOU, BUT... UH...
WHOA.

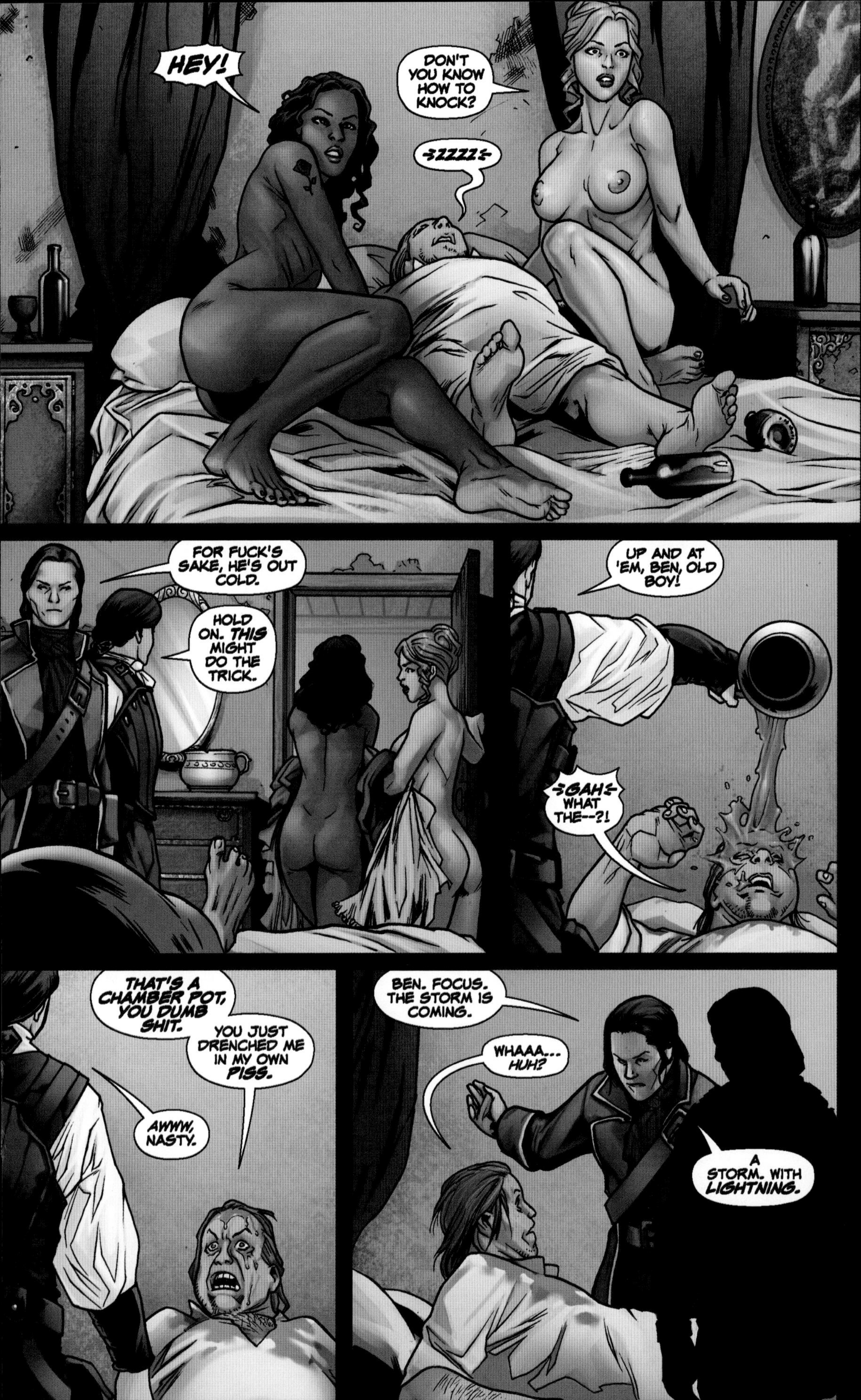
HEY!
DON'T YOU KNOW HOW TO KNOCK?
-ZZZZZ-
FOR FUCK'S SAKE, HE'S OUT COLD.
HOLD ON. THIS MIGHT DO THE TRICK.
UP AND AT 'EM, BEN, OLD BOY!
-GAH- WHAT THE--?!
THAT'S A CHAMBER POT, YOU DUMB SHIT.
YOU JUST DRENCHED ME IN MY OWN PISS.
AWWW, NASTY.
BEN. FOCUS. THE STORM IS COMING.
WHAAA... HUH?
A STORM. WITH LIGHTNING.

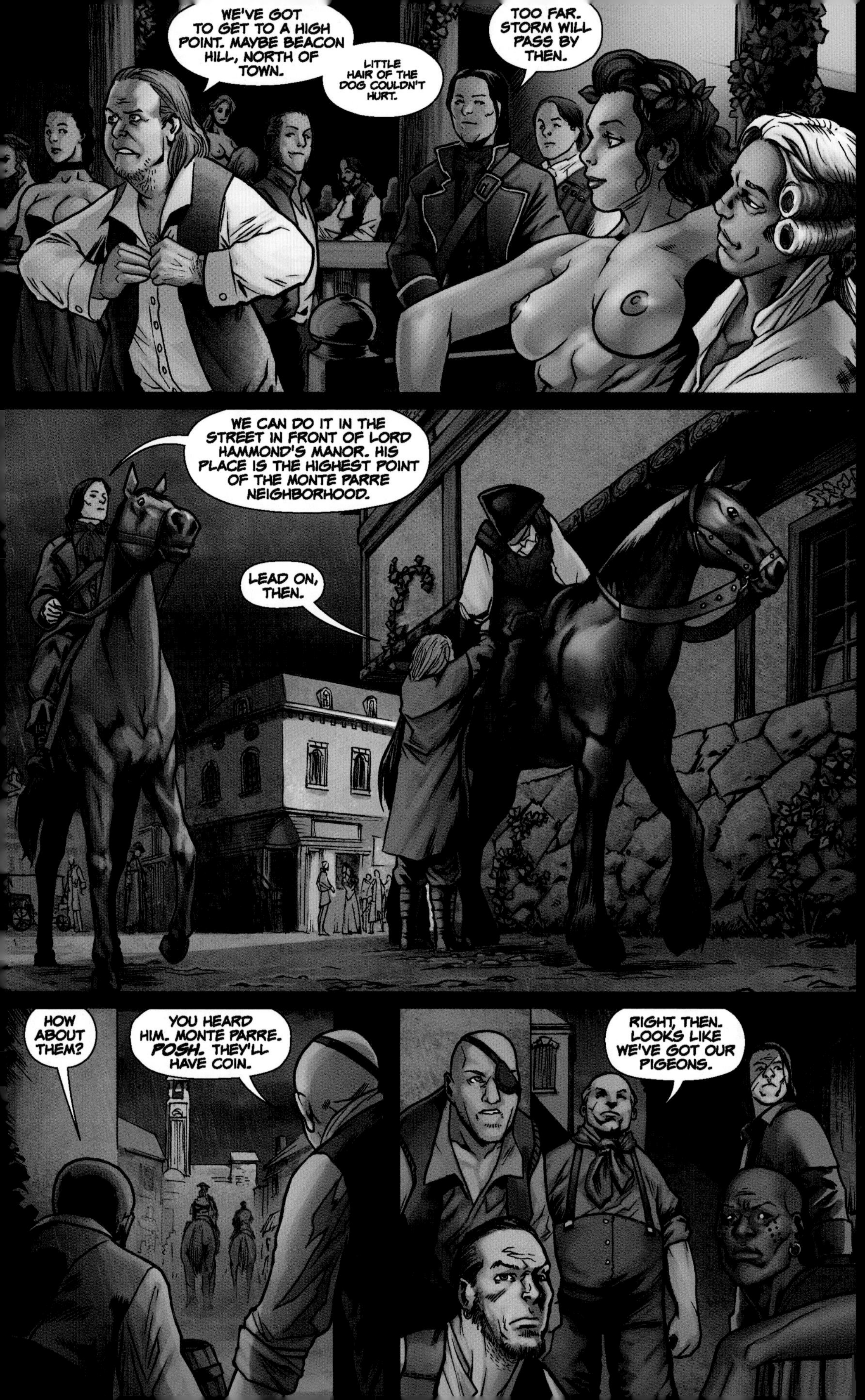
WE'VE GOT TO GET TO A HIGH POINT. MAYBE BEACON HILL, NORTH OF TOWN.
LITTLE HAIR OF THE DOG COULDN'T HURT.
TOO FAR. STORM WILL PASS BY THEN.
WE CAN DO IT IN THE STREET IN FRONT OF LORD HAMMOND'S MANOR. HIS PLACE IS THE HIGHEST POINT OF THE MONTE PARRE NEIGHBORHOOD.
LEAD ON, THEN.
HOW ABOUT THEM?
YOU HEARD HIM. MONTE PARRE. *POSH.* THEY'LL HAVE COIN.
RIGHT, THEN. LOOKS LIKE WE'VE GOT OUR PIGEONS.

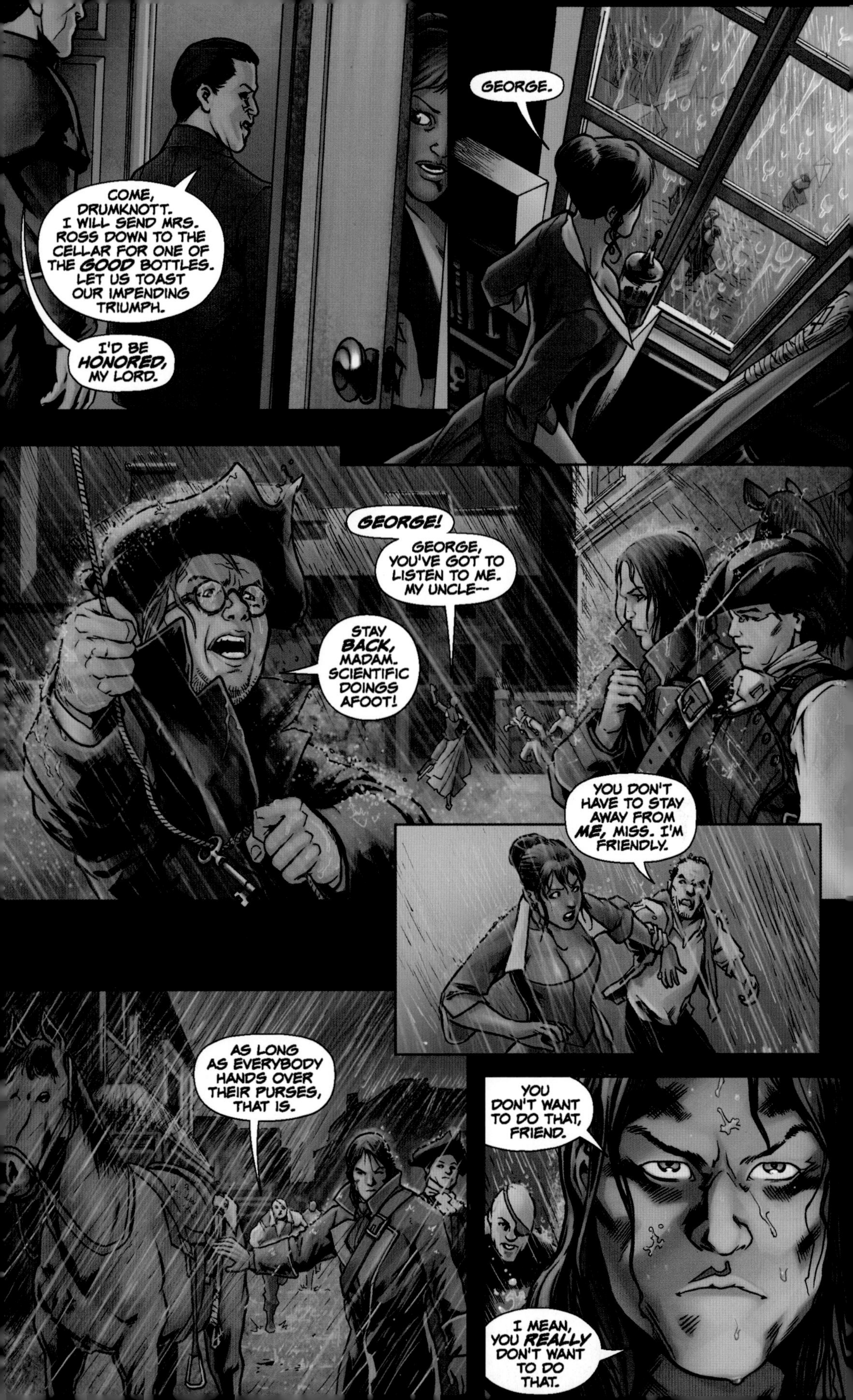
COME, DRUMKNOTT. I WILL SEND MRS. ROSS DOWN TO THE CELLAR FOR ONE OF THE GOOD BOTTLES. LET US TOAST OUR IMPENDING TRIUMPH.
I'D BE HONORED, MY LORD.
GEORGE.
GEORGE!
GEORGE, YOU'VE GOT TO LISTEN TO ME. MY UNCLE--
STAY BACK, MADAM. SCIENTIFIC DOINGS AFOOT!
YOU DON'T HAVE TO STAY AWAY FROM ME, MISS. I'M FRIENDLY.
AS LONG AS EVERYBODY HANDS OVER THEIR PURSES, THAT IS.
YOU DON'T WANT TO DO THAT, FRIEND.
I MEAN, YOU REALLY DON'T WANT TO DO THAT.

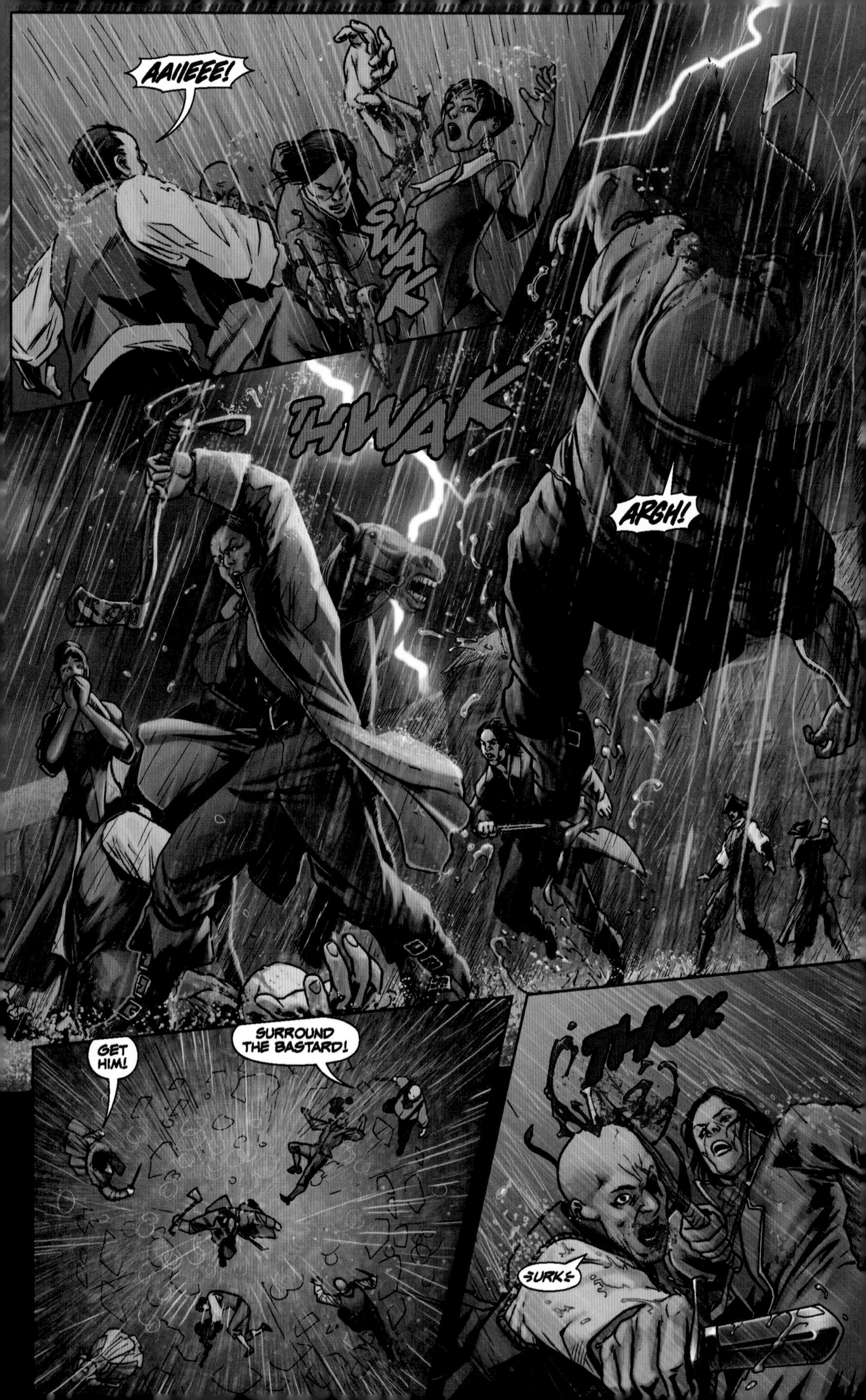
AAIIEEE!
SWAK
THWAK
ARGH!
GET HIM!
SURROUND THE BASTARD!
THOK
URK

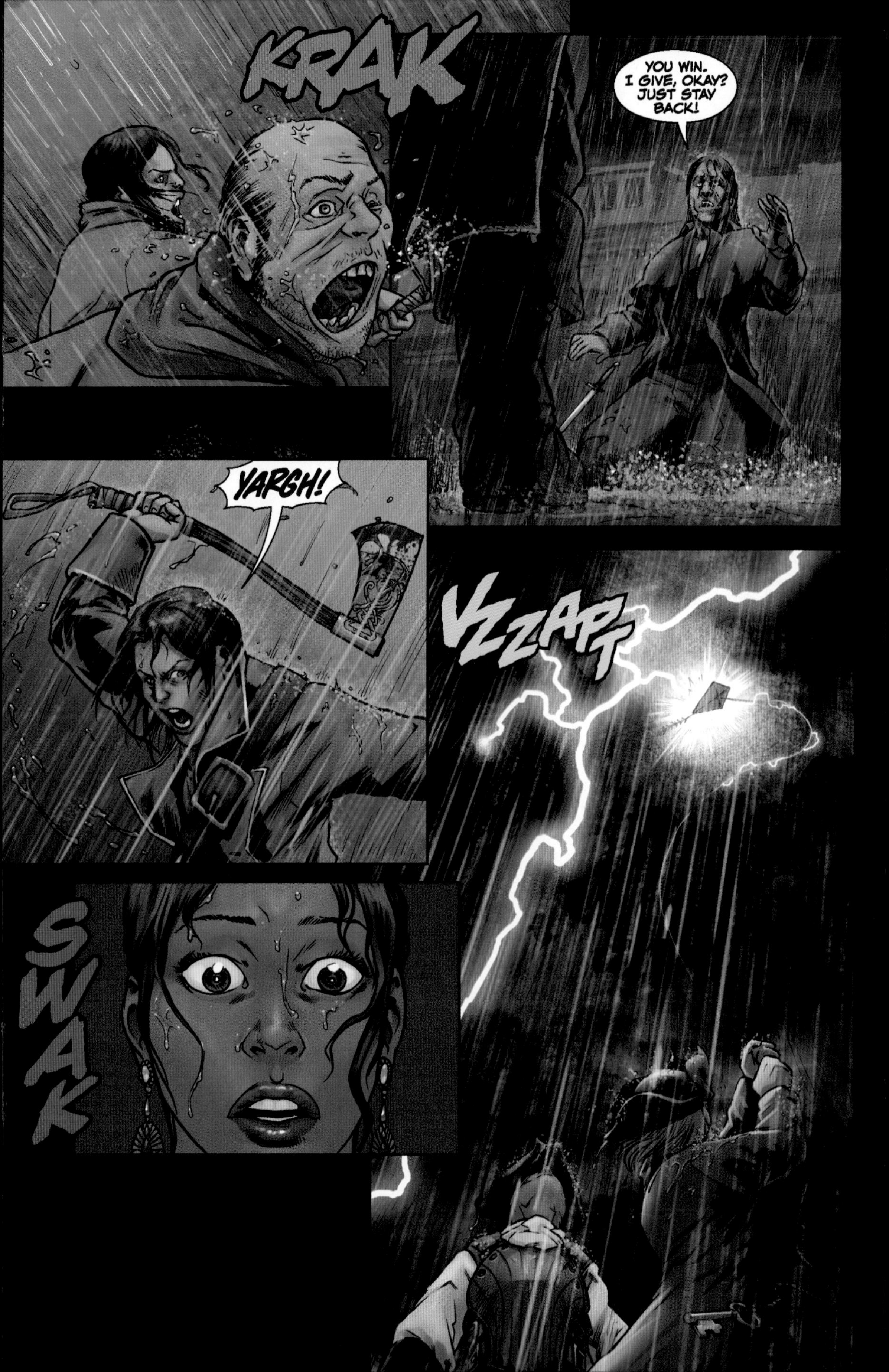
KRAK
YOU WIN. I GIVE, OKAY? JUST STAY BACK!
YARGH!
VZZAPT
SWAK

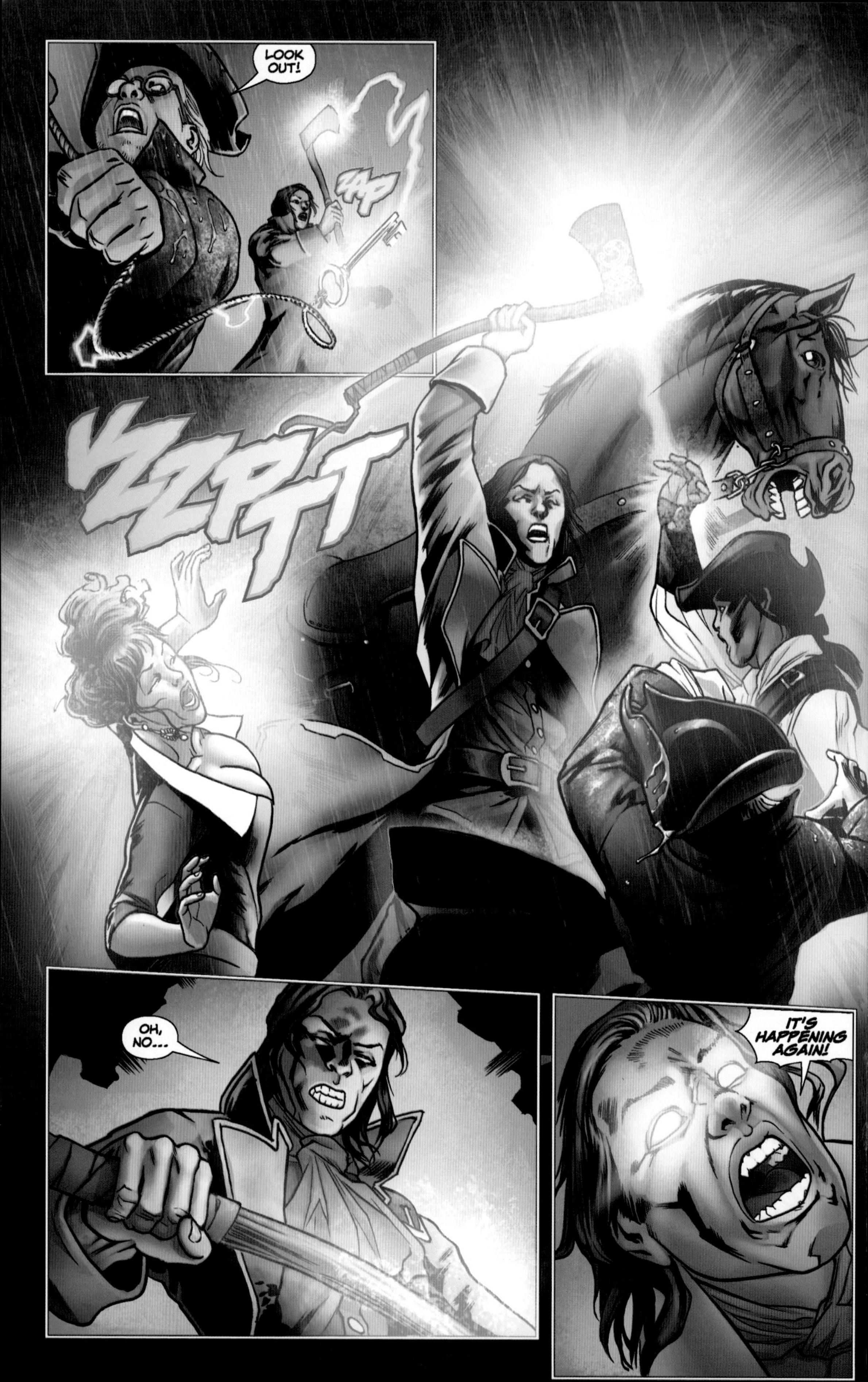
LOOK OUT!
ZAP
ZZPTT
OH, NO...
IT'S HAPPENING AGAIN!

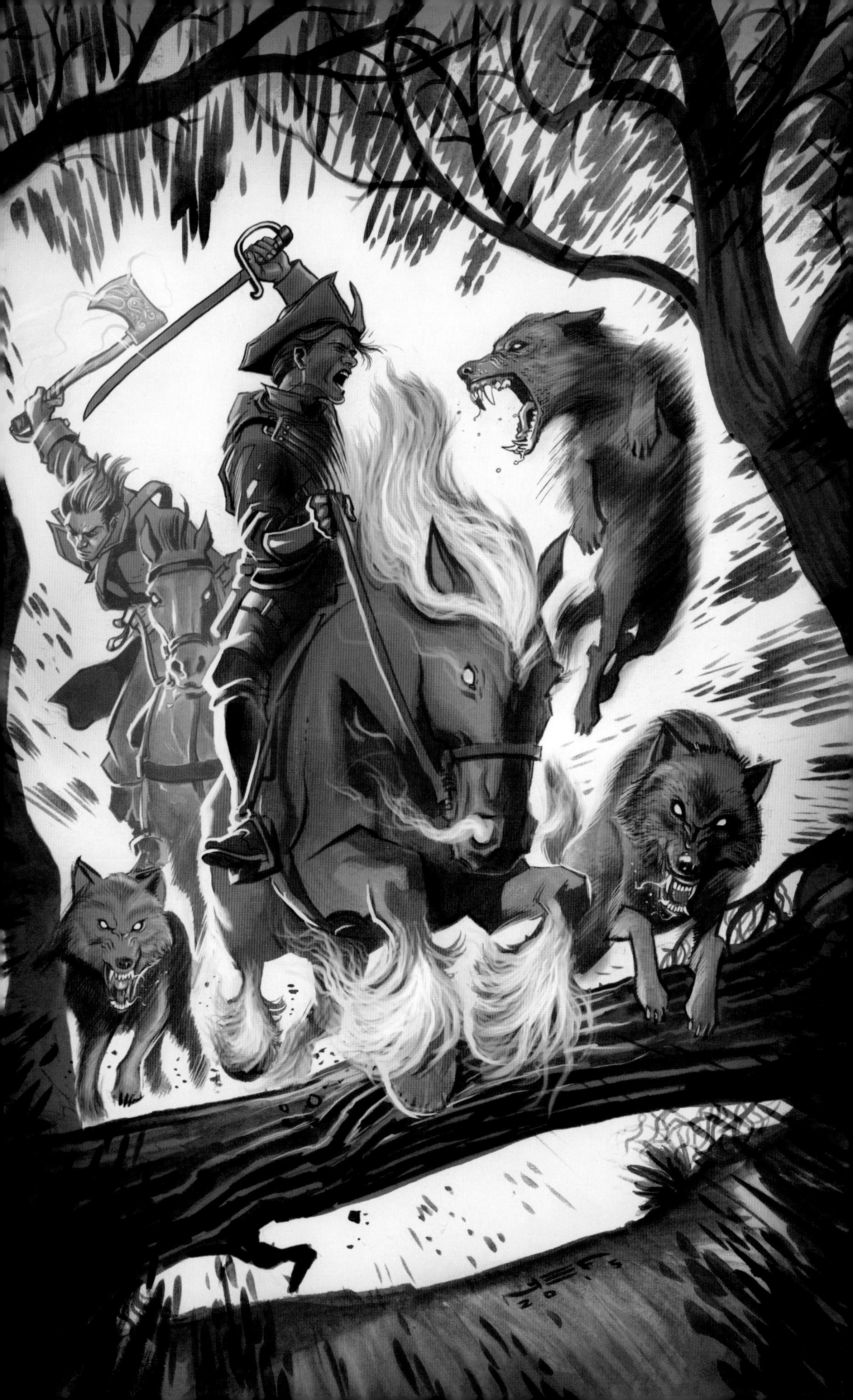

II

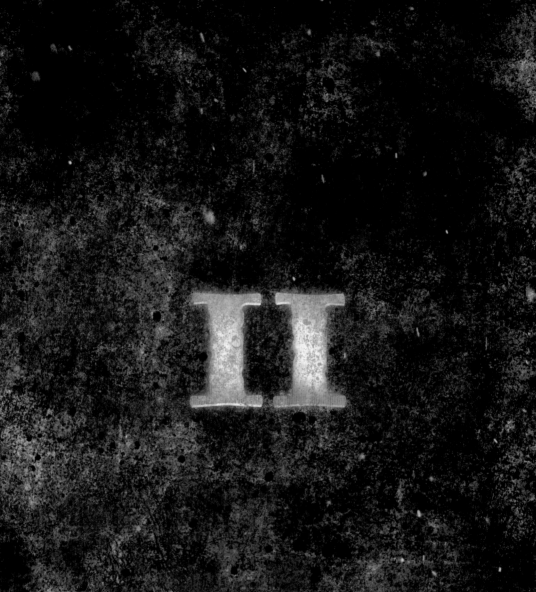

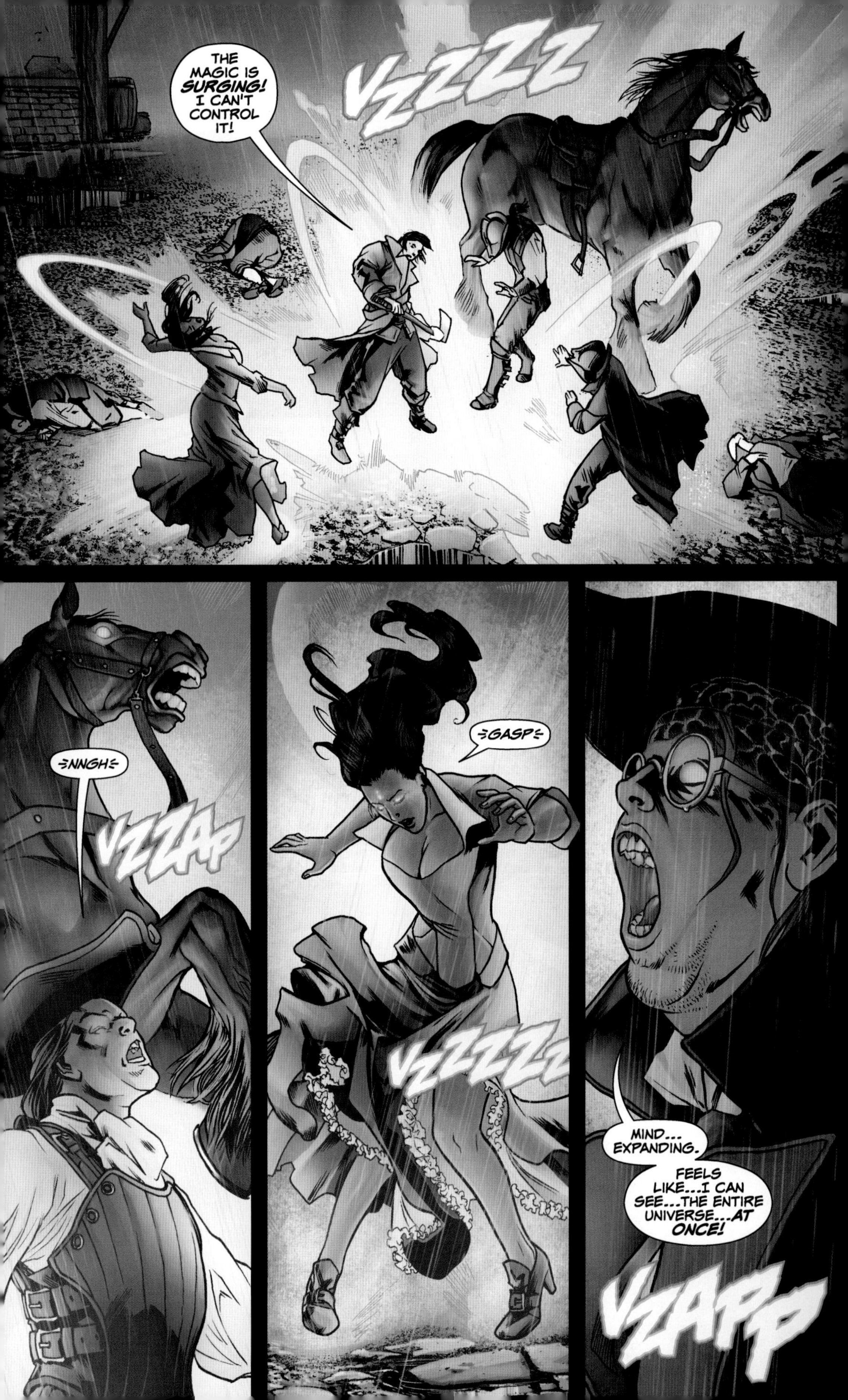
THE MAGIC IS SURGING! I CAN'T CONTROL IT!
VZZZZZ
NNGH
VZZAP
GASP
VZZZZZ
MIND... EXPANDING.
FEELS LIKE...I CAN SEE...THE ENTIRE UNIVERSE...AT ONCE!
VZAPP

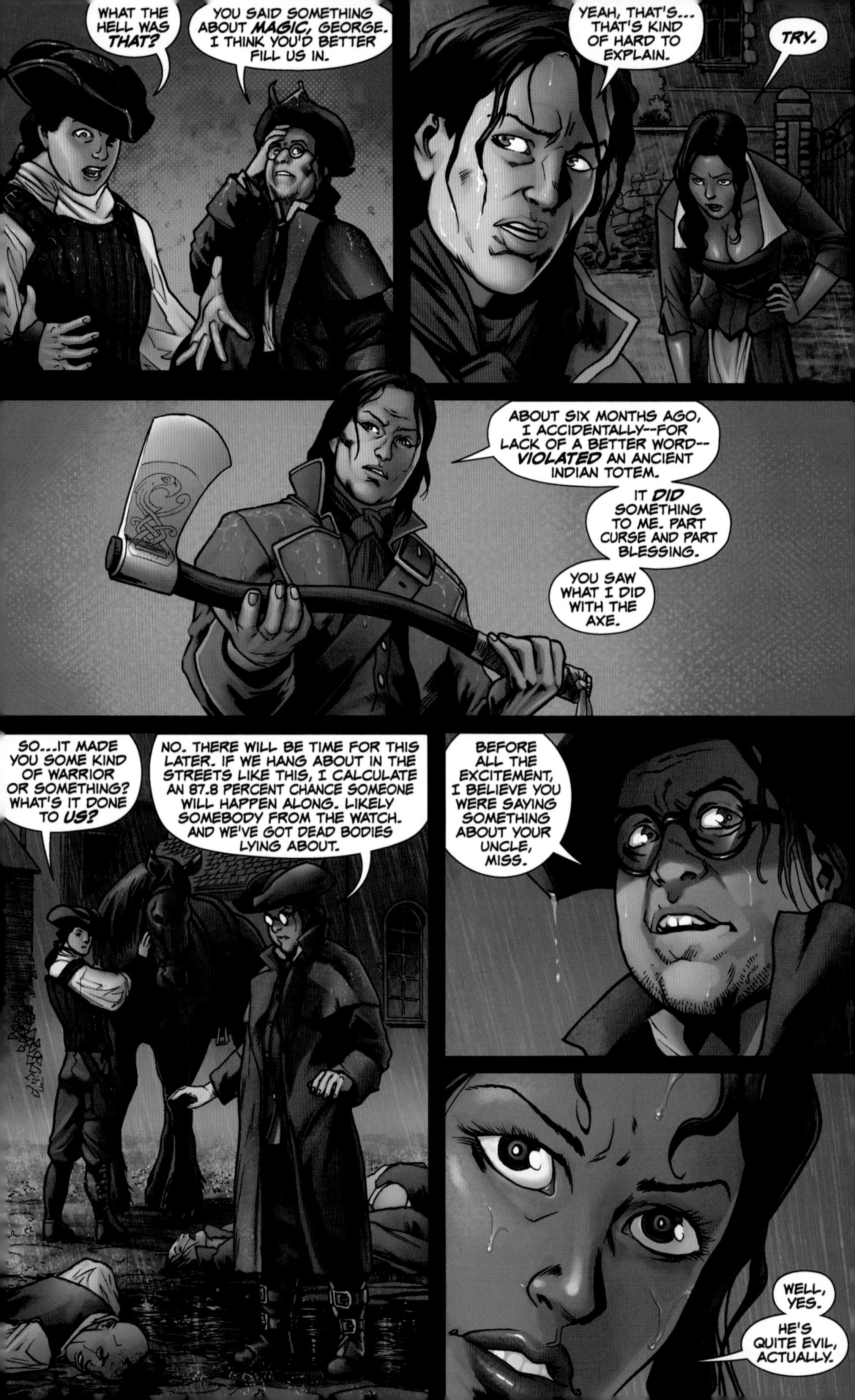
WHAT THE HELL WAS THAT?
YOU SAID SOMETHING ABOUT MAGIC, GEORGE. I THINK YOU'D BETTER FILL US IN.
YEAH, THAT'S... THAT'S KIND OF HARD TO EXPLAIN.
TRY.
ABOUT SIX MONTHS AGO, I ACCIDENTALLY--FOR LACK OF A BETTER WORD--VIOLATED AN ANCIENT INDIAN TOTEM.
IT DID SOMETHING TO ME. PART CURSE AND PART BLESSING.
YOU SAW WHAT I DID WITH THE AXE.
SO...IT MADE YOU SOME KIND OF WARRIOR OR SOMETHING? WHAT'S IT DONE TO US?
NO. THERE WILL BE TIME FOR THIS LATER. IF WE HANG ABOUT IN THE STREETS LIKE THIS, I CALCULATE AN 87.8 PERCENT CHANCE SOMEONE WILL HAPPEN ALONG. LIKELY SOMEBODY FROM THE WATCH. AND WE'VE GOT DEAD BODIES LYING ABOUT.
BEFORE ALL THE EXCITEMENT, I BELIEVE YOU WERE SAYING SOMETHING ABOUT YOUR UNCLE, MISS.
WELL, YES.
HE'S QUITE EVIL, ACTUALLY.

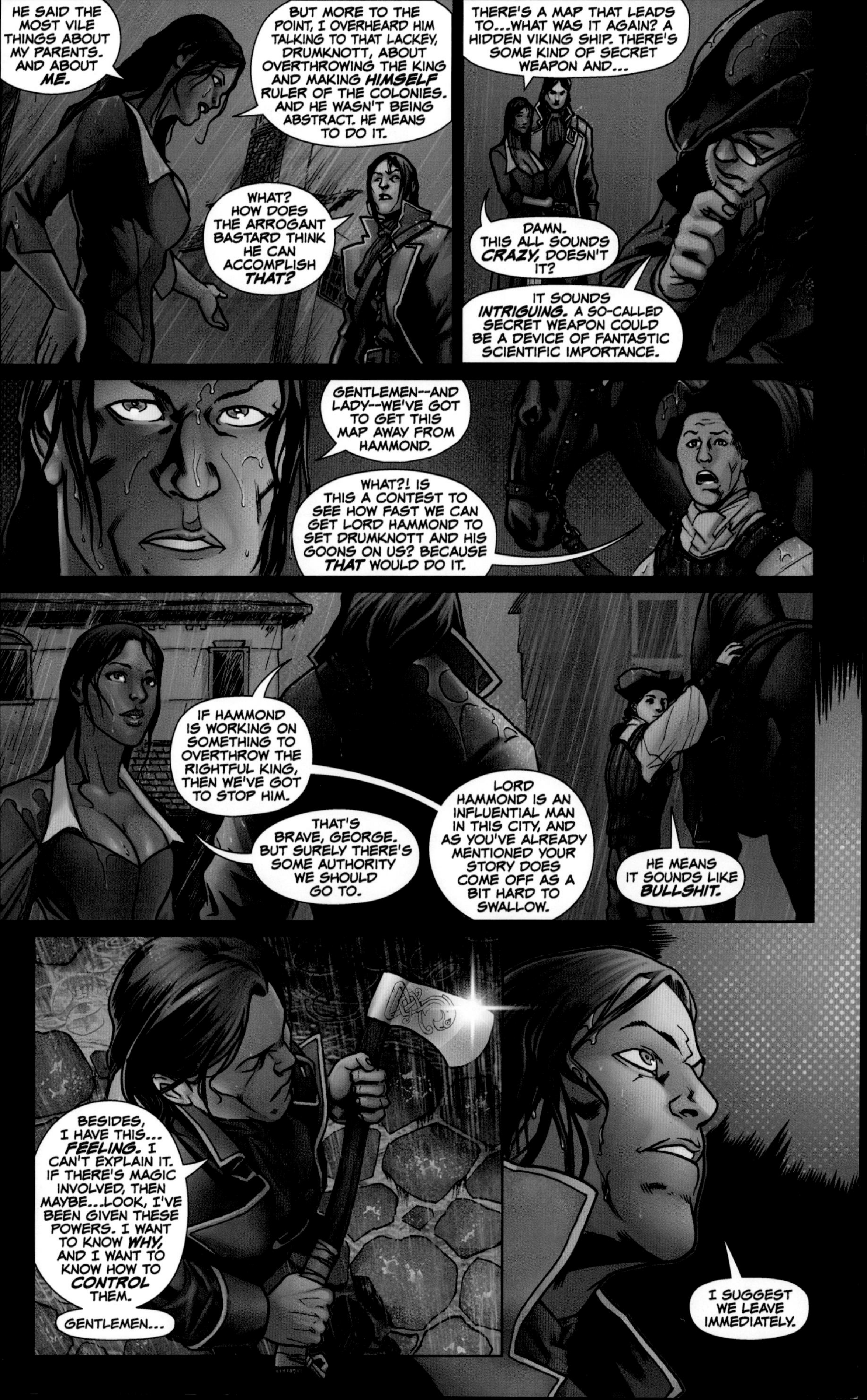
HE SAID THE MOST VILE THINGS ABOUT MY PARENTS. AND ABOUT ME.
BUT MORE TO THE POINT, I OVERHEARD HIM TALKING TO THAT LACKEY, DRUMKNOTT, ABOUT OVERTHROWING THE KING AND MAKING HIMSELF RULER OF THE COLONIES. AND HE WASN'T BEING ABSTRACT. HE MEANS TO DO IT.
WHAT? HOW DOES THE ARROGANT BASTARD THINK HE CAN ACCOMPLISH THAT?
THERE'S A MAP THAT LEADS TO...WHAT WAS IT AGAIN? A HIDDEN VIKING SHIP. THERE'S SOME KIND OF SECRET WEAPON AND...
DAMN. THIS ALL SOUNDS CRAZY, DOESN'T IT?
IT SOUNDS INTRIGUING. A SO-CALLED SECRET WEAPON COULD BE A DEVICE OF FANTASTIC SCIENTIFIC IMPORTANCE.
GENTLEMEN--AND LADY--WE'VE GOT TO GET THIS MAP AWAY FROM HAMMOND.
WHAT?! IS THIS A CONTEST TO SEE HOW FAST WE CAN GET LORD HAMMOND TO SET DRUMKNOTT AND HIS GOONS ON US? BECAUSE THAT WOULD DO IT.
IF HAMMOND IS WORKING ON SOMETHING TO OVERTHROW THE RIGHTFUL KING, THEN WE'VE GOT TO STOP HIM.
THAT'S BRAVE, GEORGE. BUT SURELY THERE'S SOME AUTHORITY WE SHOULD GO TO.
LORD HAMMOND IS AN INFLUENTIAL MAN IN THIS CITY, AND AS YOU'VE ALREADY MENTIONED YOUR STORY DOES COME OFF AS A BIT HARD TO SWALLOW.
HE MEANS IT SOUNDS LIKE BULLSHIT.
BESIDES, I HAVE THIS... FEELING. I CAN'T EXPLAIN IT. IF THERE'S MAGIC INVOLVED, THEN MAYBE...LOOK, I'VE BEEN GIVEN THESE POWERS. I WANT TO KNOW WHY, AND I WANT TO KNOW HOW TO CONTROL THEM.
GENTLEMEN...
I SUGGEST WE LEAVE IMMEDIATELY.

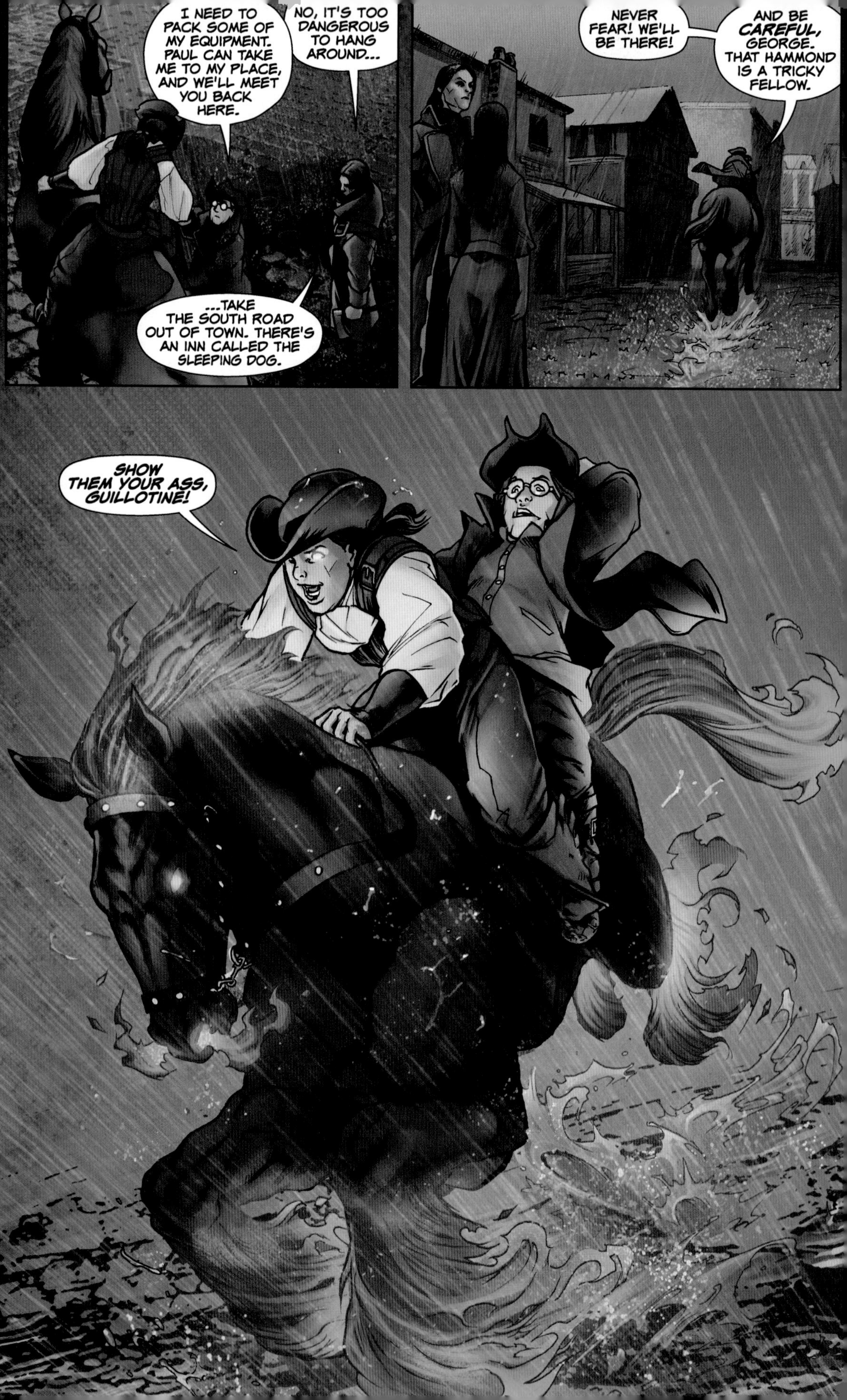
I NEED TO PACK SOME OF MY EQUIPMENT. PAUL CAN TAKE ME TO MY PLACE, AND WE'LL MEET YOU BACK HERE.
NO, IT'S TOO DANGEROUS TO HANG AROUND...
...TAKE THE SOUTH ROAD OUT OF TOWN. THERE'S AN INN CALLED THE SLEEPING DOG.
NEVER FEAR! WE'LL BE THERE!
AND BE CAREFUL, GEORGE. THAT HAMMOND IS A TRICKY FELLOW.
SHOW THEM YOUR ASS, GUILLOTINE!

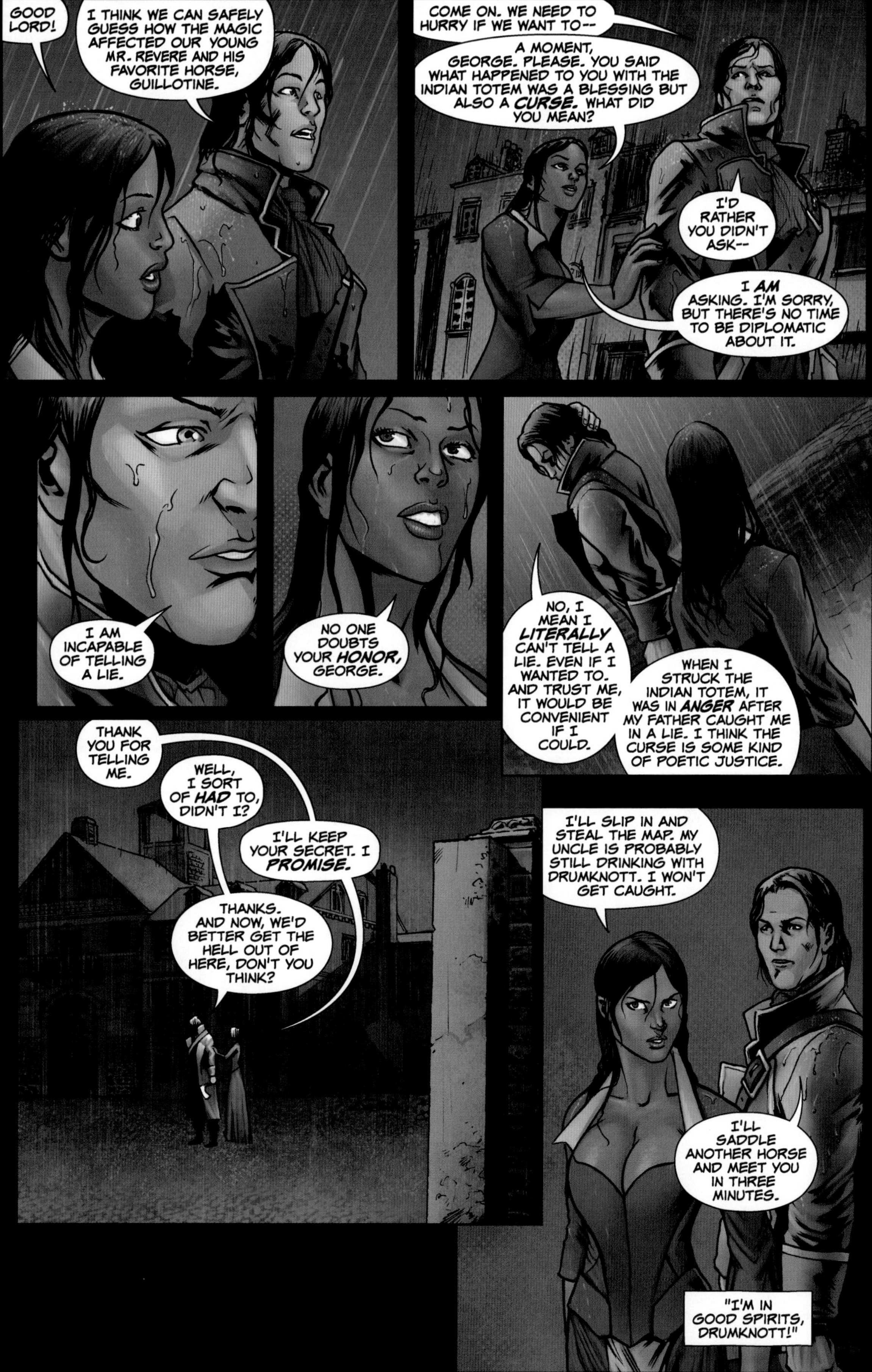
GOOD LORD!
I THINK WE CAN SAFELY GUESS HOW THE MAGIC AFFECTED OUR YOUNG MR. REVERE AND HIS FAVORITE HORSE, GUILLOTINE.
COME ON. WE NEED TO HURRY IF WE WANT TO--
A MOMENT, GEORGE. PLEASE. YOU SAID WHAT HAPPENED TO YOU WITH THE INDIAN TOTEM WAS A BLESSING BUT ALSO A CURSE. WHAT DID YOU MEAN?
I'D RATHER YOU DIDN'T ASK--
I AM ASKING. I'M SORRY, BUT THERE'S NO TIME TO BE DIPLOMATIC ABOUT IT.
I AM INCAPABLE OF TELLING A LIE.
NO ONE DOUBTS YOUR HONOR, GEORGE.
NO, I MEAN I LITERALLY CAN'T TELL A LIE. EVEN IF I WANTED TO. AND TRUST ME, IT WOULD BE CONVENIENT IF I COULD.
WHEN I STRUCK THE INDIAN TOTEM, IT WAS IN ANGER AFTER MY FATHER CAUGHT ME IN A LIE. I THINK THE CURSE IS SOME KIND OF POETIC JUSTICE.
THANK YOU FOR TELLING ME.
WELL, I SORT OF HAD TO, DIDN'T I?
I'LL KEEP YOUR SECRET. I PROMISE.
THANKS. AND NOW, WE'D BETTER GET THE HELL OUT OF HERE, DON'T YOU THINK?
I'LL SLIP IN AND STEAL THE MAP. MY UNCLE IS PROBABLY STILL DRINKING WITH DRUMKNOTT. I WON'T GET CAUGHT.
I'LL SADDLE ANOTHER HORSE AND MEET YOU IN THREE MINUTES.
"I'M IN GOOD SPIRITS, DRUMKNOTT!"

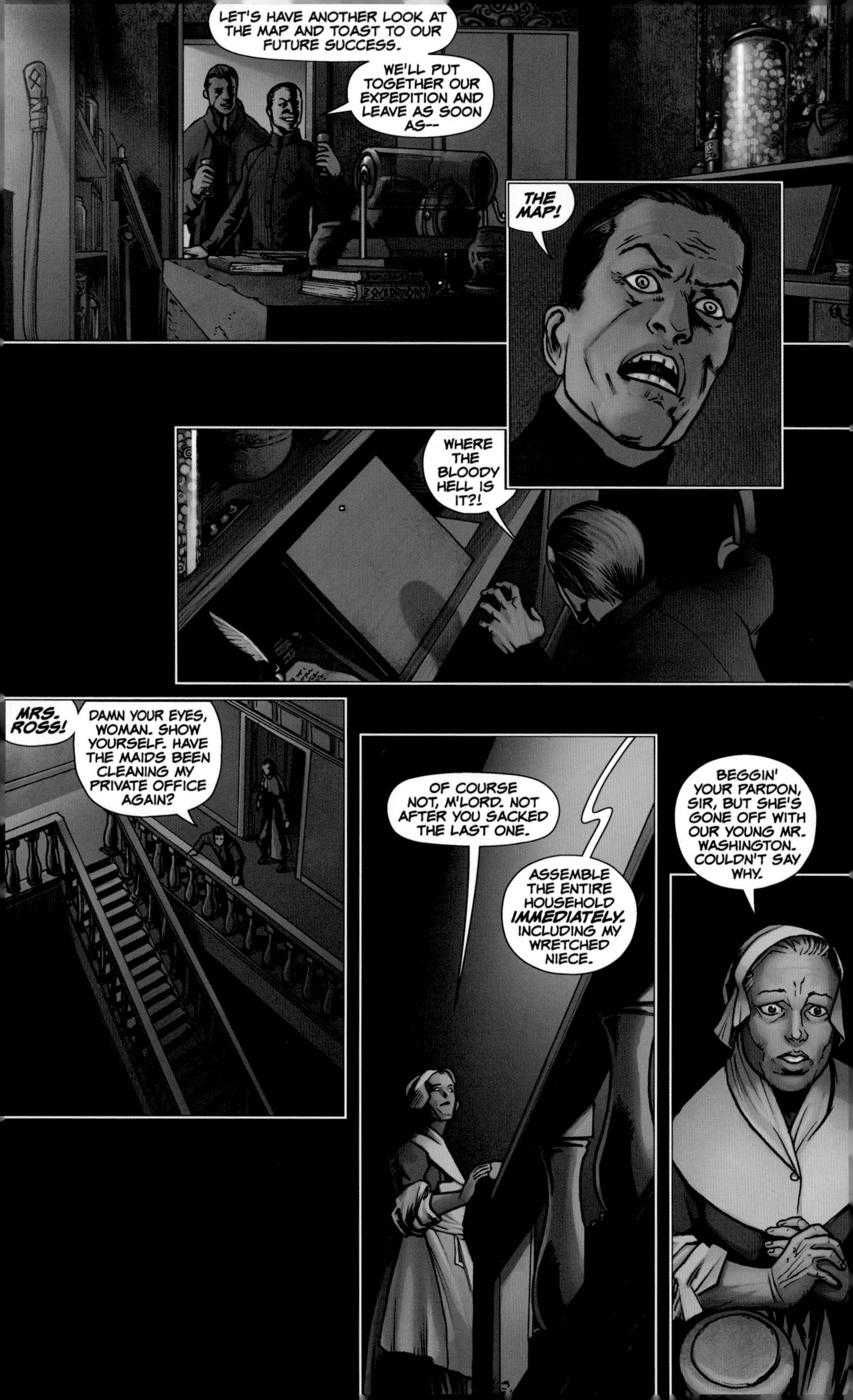
LET'S HAVE ANOTHER LOOK AT THE MAP AND TOAST TO OUR FUTURE SUCCESS.
WE'LL PUT TOGETHER OUR EXPEDITION AND LEAVE AS SOON AS--
THE MAP!
WHERE THE BLOODY HELL IS IT?!
MRS. ROSS!
DAMN YOUR EYES, WOMAN. SHOW YOURSELF. HAVE THE MAIDS BEEN CLEANING MY PRIVATE OFFICE AGAIN?
OF COURSE NOT, M'LORD. NOT AFTER YOU SACKED THE LAST ONE.
ASSEMBLE THE ENTIRE HOUSEHOLD IMMEDIATELY. INCLUDING MY WRETCHED NIECE.
BEGGIN' YOUR PARDON, SIR, BUT SHE'S GONE OFF WITH OUR YOUNG MR. WASHINGTON. COULDN'T SAY WHY.

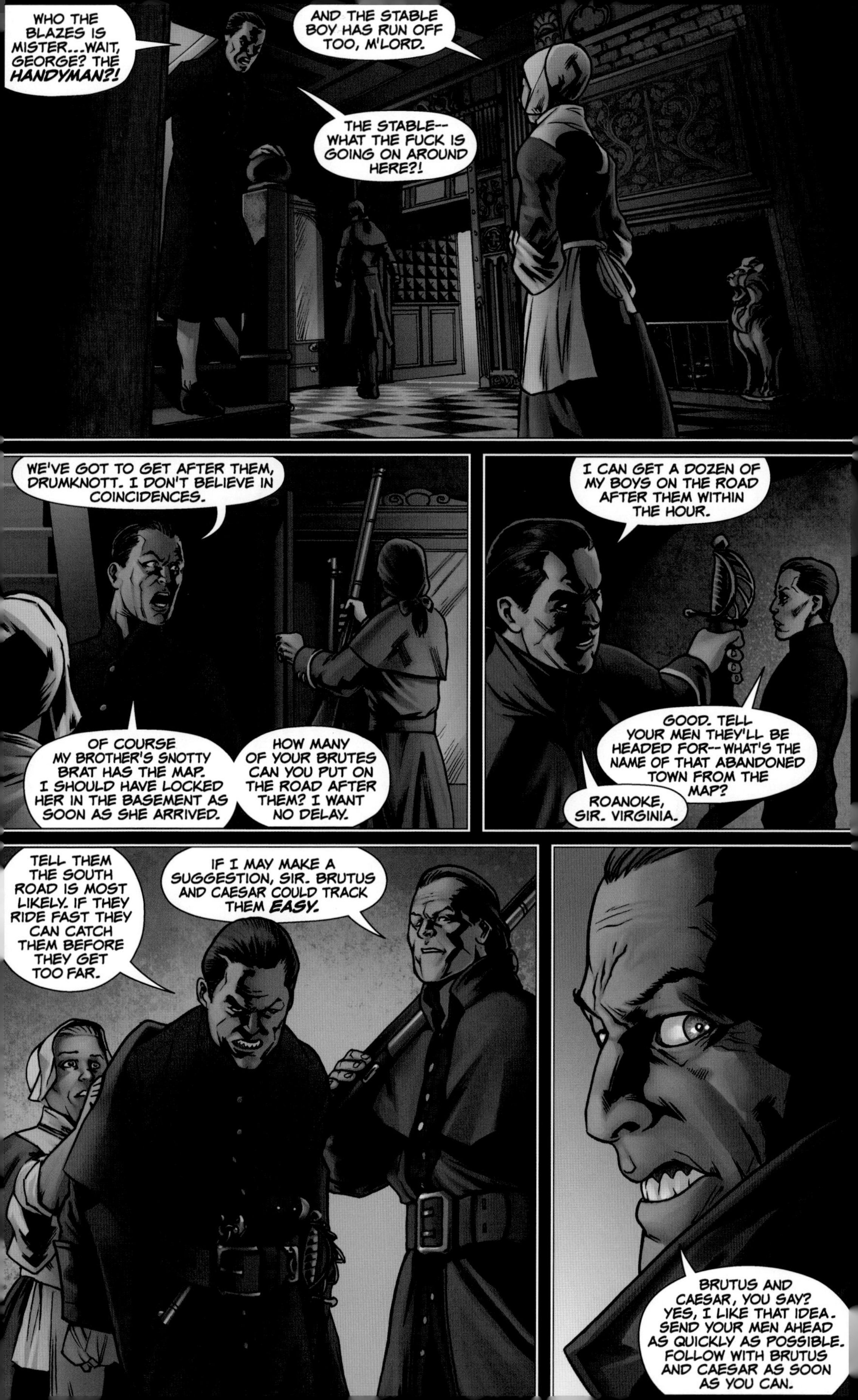
WHO THE BLAZES IS MISTER...WAIT, GEORGE? THE *HANDYMAN?!*
AND THE STABLE BOY HAS RUN OFF TOO, M'LORD.
THE STABLE-- WHAT THE FUCK IS GOING ON AROUND HERE?!
WE'VE GOT TO GET AFTER THEM, DRUMKNOTT. I DON'T BELIEVE IN COINCIDENCES.
OF COURSE MY BROTHER'S SNOTTY BRAT HAS THE MAP. I SHOULD HAVE LOCKED HER IN THE BASEMENT AS SOON AS SHE ARRIVED.
HOW MANY OF YOUR BRUTES CAN YOU PUT ON THE ROAD AFTER THEM? I WANT NO DELAY.
I CAN GET A DOZEN OF MY BOYS ON THE ROAD AFTER THEM WITHIN THE HOUR.
GOOD. TELL YOUR MEN THEY'LL BE HEADED FOR--WHAT'S THE NAME OF THAT ABANDONED TOWN FROM THE MAP?
ROANOKE, SIR. VIRGINIA.
TELL THEM THE SOUTH ROAD IS MOST LIKELY. IF THEY RIDE FAST THEY CAN CATCH THEM BEFORE THEY GET TOO FAR.
IF I MAY MAKE A SUGGESTION, SIR. BRUTUS AND CAESAR COULD TRACK THEM *EASY.*
BRUTUS AND CAESAR, YOU SAY? YES, I LIKE THAT IDEA. SEND YOUR MEN AHEAD AS QUICKLY AS POSSIBLE. FOLLOW WITH BRUTUS AND CAESAR AS SOON AS YOU CAN.

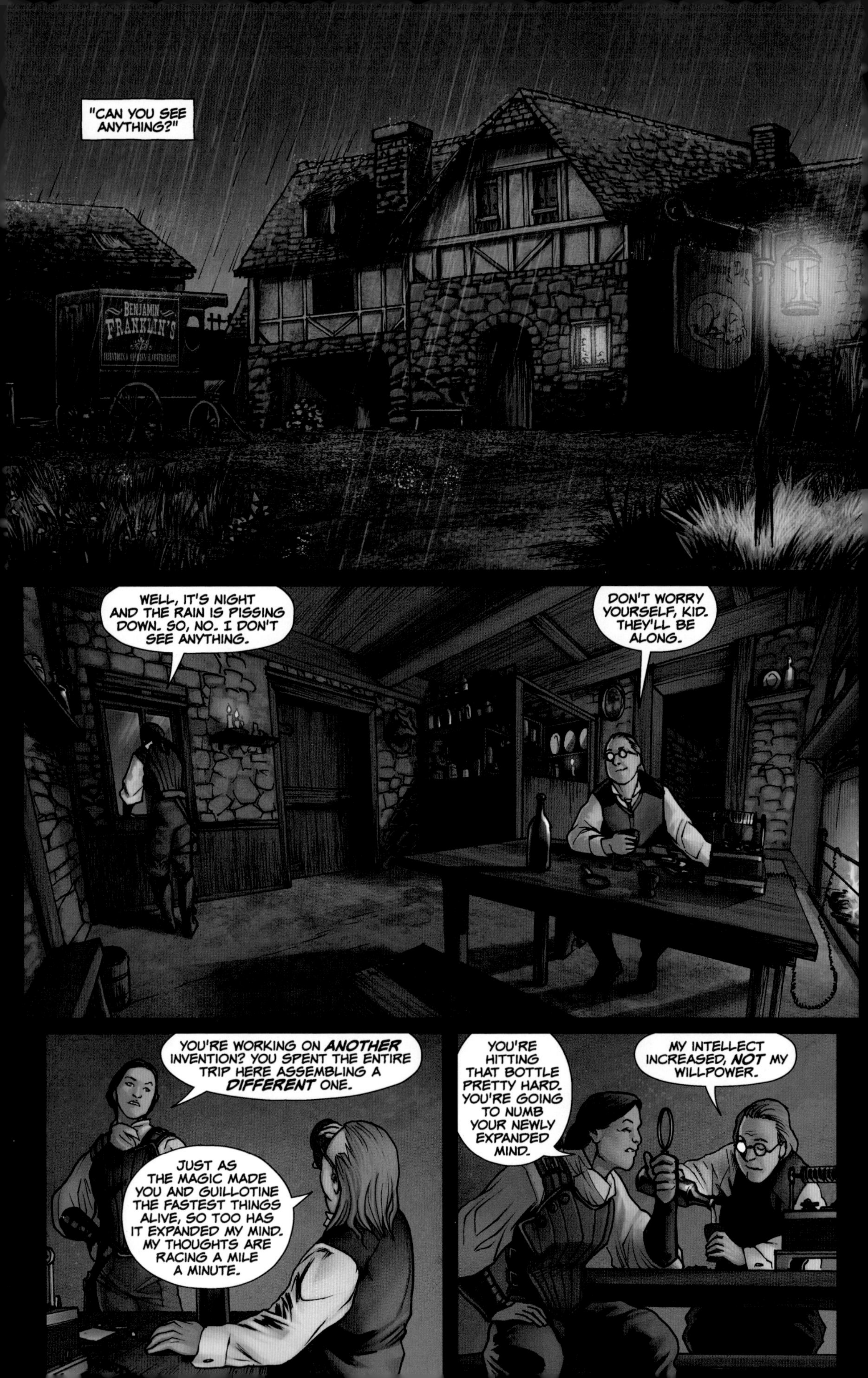
"CAN YOU SEE ANYTHING?"
BENJAMIN FRANKLIN'S
WELL, IT'S NIGHT AND THE RAIN IS PISSING DOWN. SO, NO. I DON'T SEE ANYTHING.
DON'T WORRY YOURSELF, KID. THEY'LL BE ALONG.
YOU'RE WORKING ON ANOTHER INVENTION? YOU SPENT THE ENTIRE TRIP HERE ASSEMBLING A DIFFERENT ONE.
JUST AS THE MAGIC MADE YOU AND GUILLOTINE THE FASTEST THINGS ALIVE, SO TOO HAS IT EXPANDED MY MIND. MY THOUGHTS ARE RACING A MILE A MINUTE.
YOU'RE HITTING THAT BOTTLE PRETTY HARD. YOU'RE GOING TO NUMB YOUR NEWLY EXPANDED MIND.
MY INTELLECT INCREASED, NOT MY WILLPOWER.

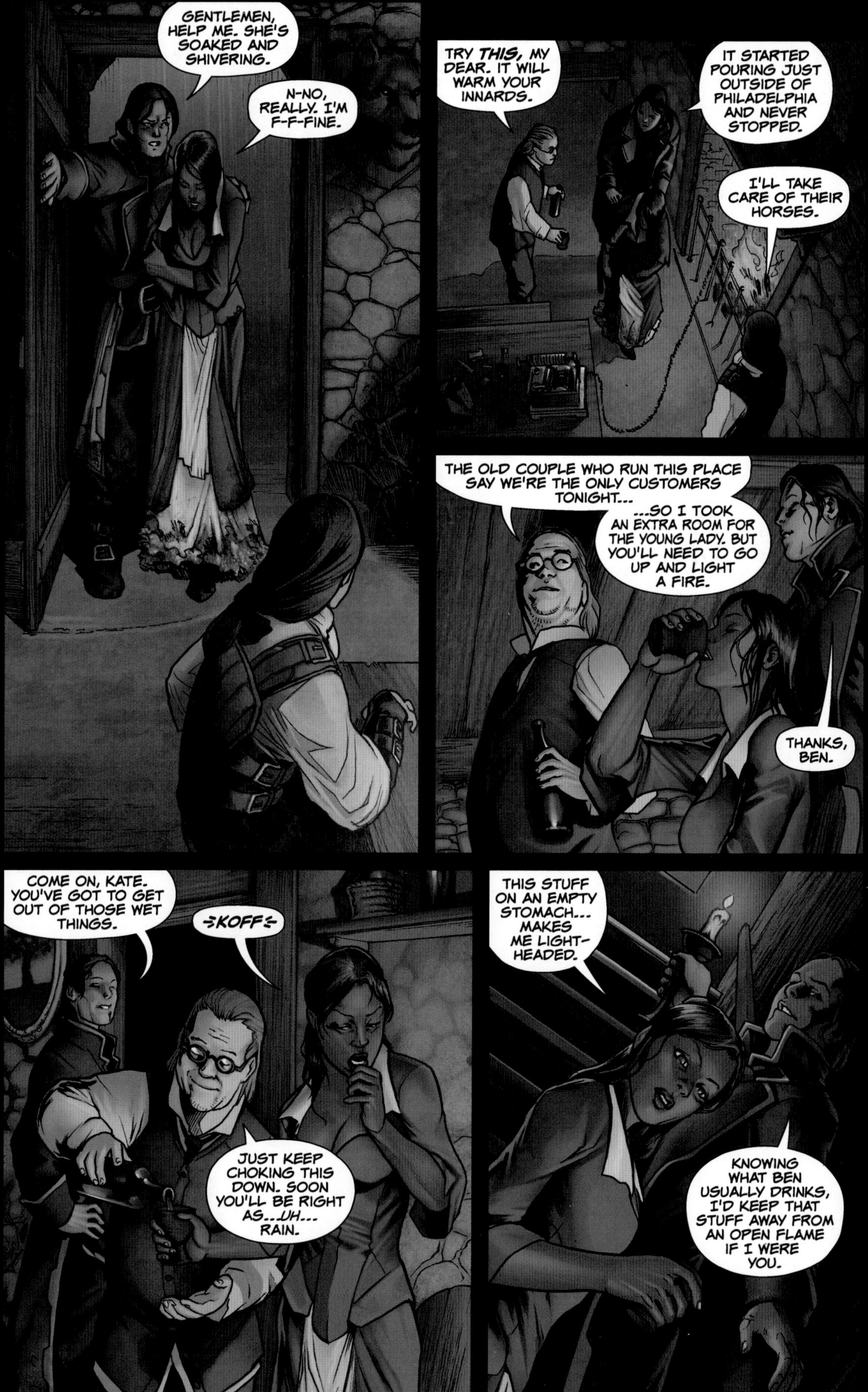
GENTLEMEN, HELP ME. SHE'S SOAKED AND SHIVERING.
N-NO, REALLY. I'M F-F-FINE.
TRY THIS, MY DEAR. IT WILL WARM YOUR INNARDS.
IT STARTED POURING JUST OUTSIDE OF PHILADELPHIA AND NEVER STOPPED.
I'LL TAKE CARE OF THEIR HORSES.
THE OLD COUPLE WHO RUN THIS PLACE SAY WE'RE THE ONLY CUSTOMERS TONIGHT...
...SO I TOOK AN EXTRA ROOM FOR THE YOUNG LADY. BUT YOU'LL NEED TO GO UP AND LIGHT A FIRE.
THANKS, BEN.
COME ON, KATE. YOU'VE GOT TO GET OUT OF THOSE WET THINGS.
KOFF
JUST KEEP CHOKING THIS DOWN. SOON YOU'LL BE RIGHT AS...UH... RAIN.
THIS STUFF ON AN EMPTY STOMACH... MAKES ME LIGHT-HEADED.
KNOWING WHAT BEN USUALLY DRINKS, I'D KEEP THAT STUFF AWAY FROM AN OPEN FLAME IF I WERE YOU.

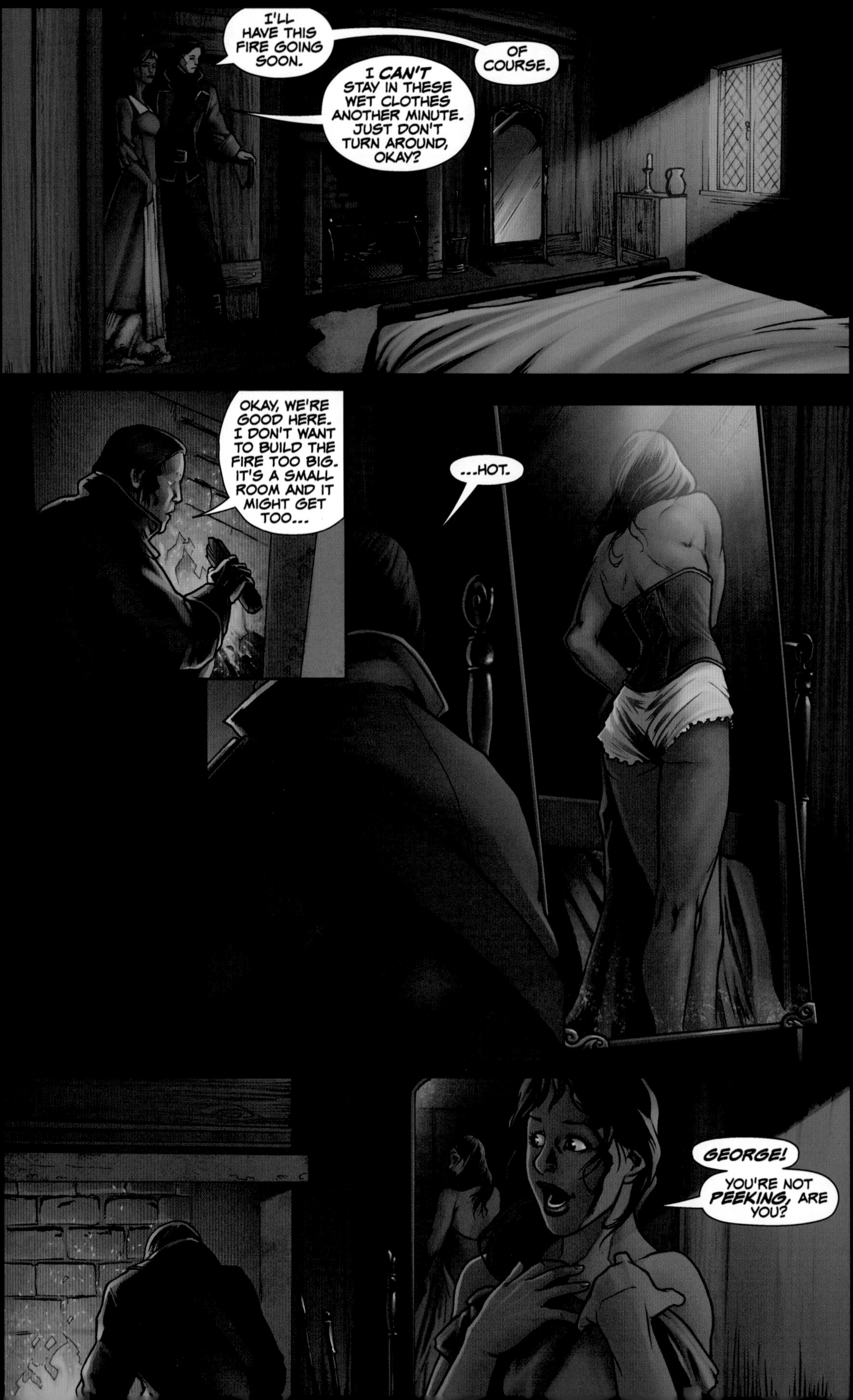
I'LL HAVE THIS FIRE GOING SOON.
OF COURSE.
I CAN'T STAY IN THESE WET CLOTHES ANOTHER MINUTE. JUST DON'T TURN AROUND, OKAY?
OKAY, WE'RE GOOD HERE. I DON'T WANT TO BUILD THE FIRE TOO BIG. IT'S A SMALL ROOM AND IT MIGHT GET TOO...
...HOT.
GEORGE!
YOU'RE NOT PEEKING, ARE YOU?

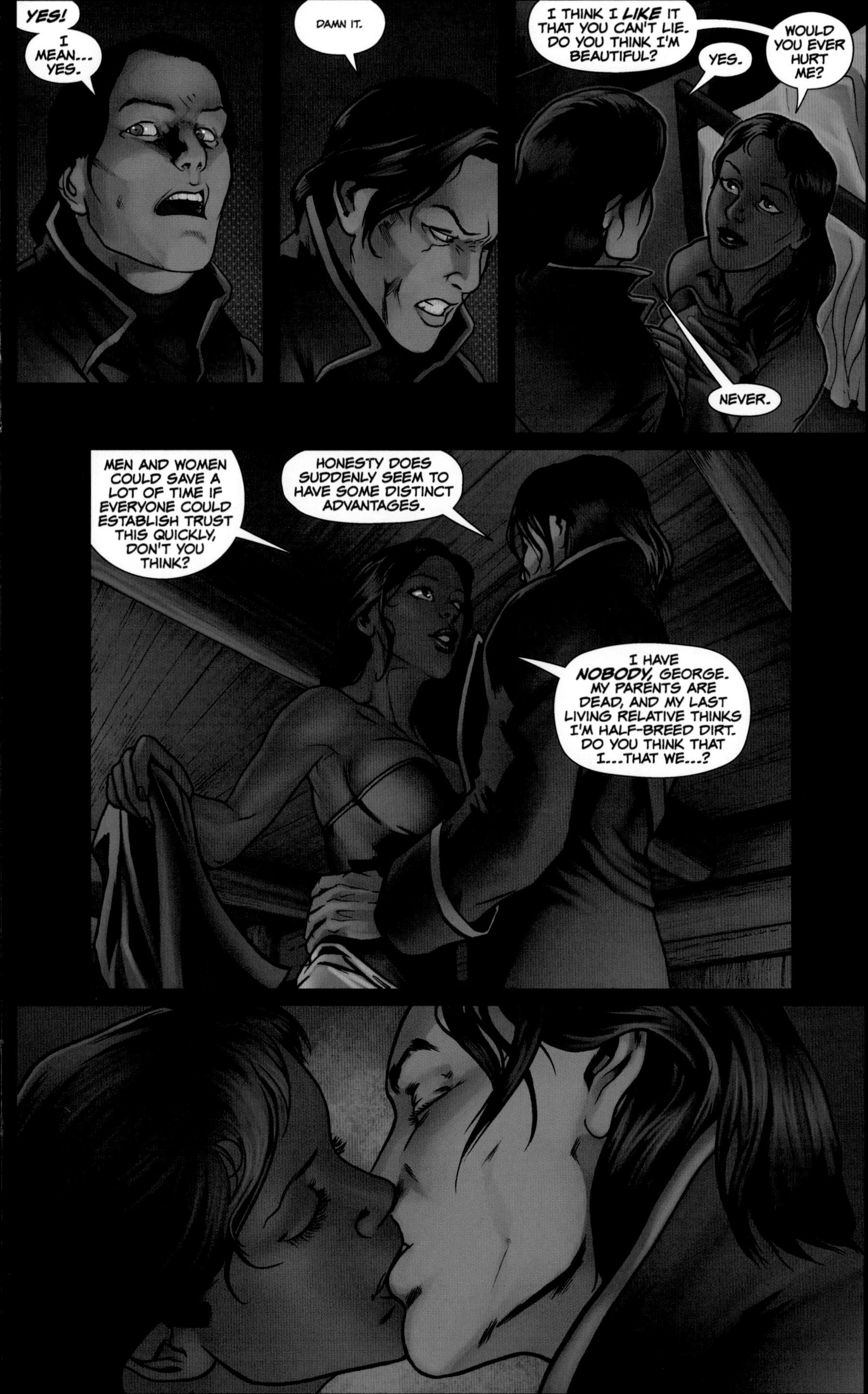
YES! I MEAN... YES.
DAMN IT.
I THINK I LIKE IT THAT YOU CAN'T LIE. DO YOU THINK I'M BEAUTIFUL?
YES.
WOULD YOU EVER HURT ME?
NEVER.
MEN AND WOMEN COULD SAVE A LOT OF TIME IF EVERYONE COULD ESTABLISH TRUST THIS QUICKLY, DON'T YOU THINK?
HONESTY DOES SUDDENLY SEEM TO HAVE SOME DISTINCT ADVANTAGES.
I HAVE NOBODY, GEORGE. MY PARENTS ARE DEAD, AND MY LAST LIVING RELATIVE THINKS I'M HALF-BREED DIRT. DO YOU THINK THAT I...THAT WE...?

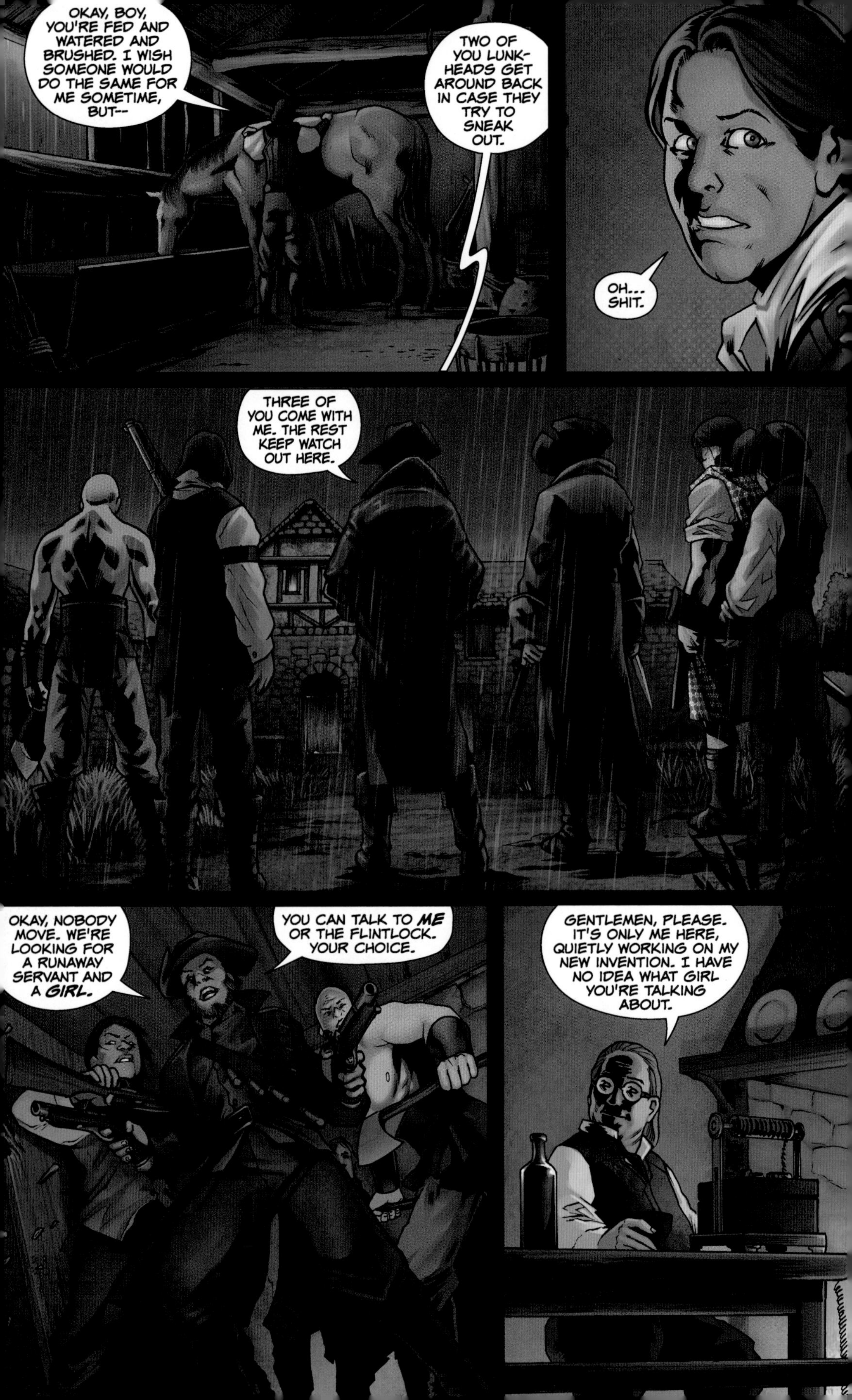
OKAY, BOY, YOU'RE FED AND WATERED AND BRUSHED. I WISH SOMEONE WOULD DO THE SAME FOR ME SOMETIME, BUT--
TWO OF YOU LUNK-HEADS GET AROUND BACK IN CASE THEY TRY TO SNEAK OUT.
OH... SHIT.
THREE OF YOU COME WITH ME. THE REST KEEP WATCH OUT HERE.
OKAY, NOBODY MOVE. WE'RE LOOKING FOR A RUNAWAY SERVANT AND A *GIRL*.
YOU CAN TALK TO *ME* OR THE FLINTLOCK. YOUR CHOICE.
GENTLEMEN, PLEASE. IT'S ONLY ME HERE, QUIETLY WORKING ON MY NEW INVENTION. I HAVE NO IDEA WHAT GIRL YOU'RE TALKING ABOUT.

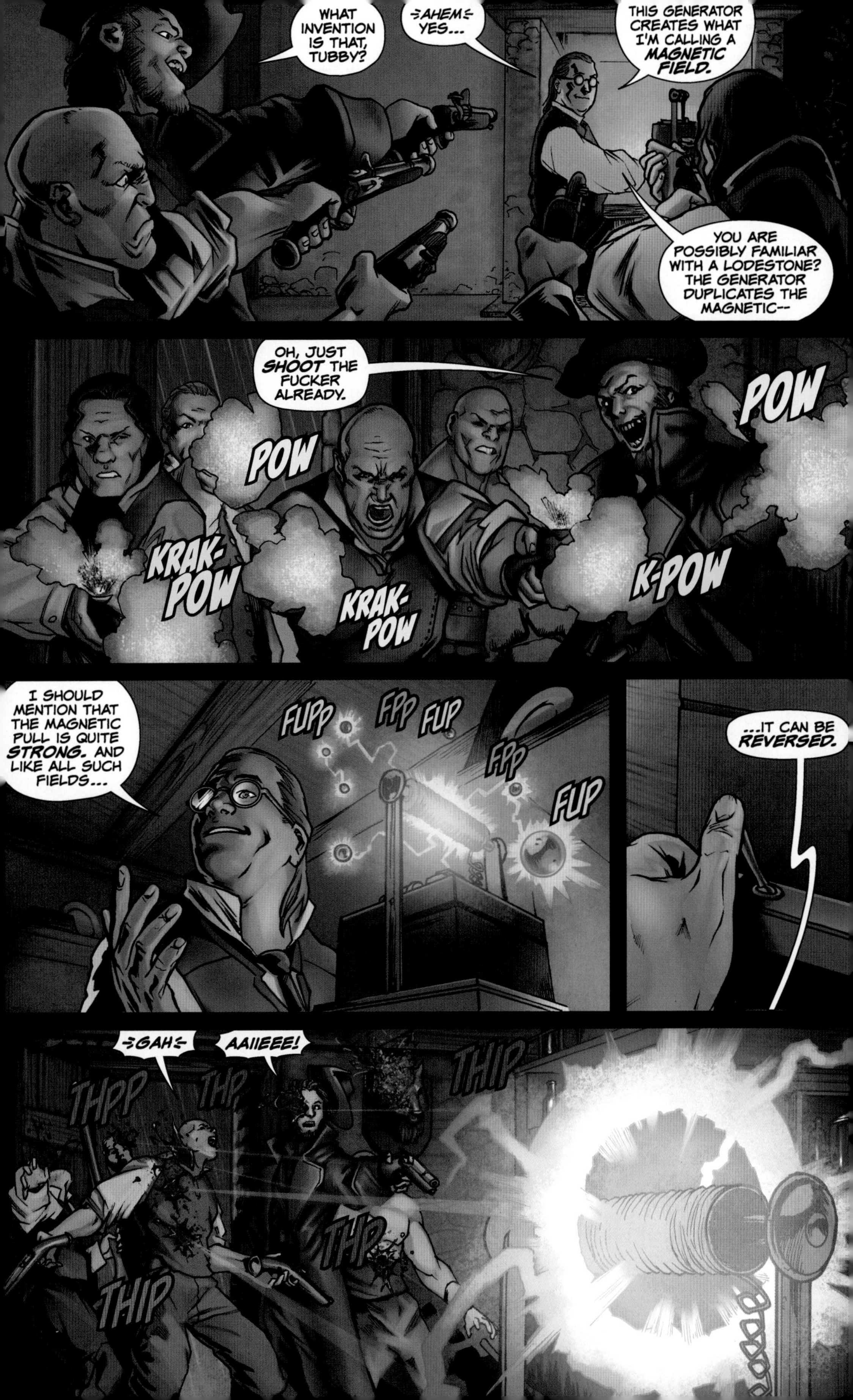
WHAT INVENTION IS THAT, TUBBY?
AHEM YES...
THIS GENERATOR CREATES WHAT I'M CALLING A MAGNETIC FIELD.
YOU ARE POSSIBLY FAMILIAR WITH A LODESTONE? THE GENERATOR DUPLICATES THE MAGNETIC--
OH, JUST SHOOT THE FUCKER ALREADY.
POW
KRAK-POW
KRAK-POW
K-POW
POW
I SHOULD MENTION THAT THE MAGNETIC PULL IS QUITE STRONG. AND LIKE ALL SUCH FIELDS...
FUPP
FPP
FUP
FPP
FUP
...IT CAN BE REVERSED.
GAH
AAIIEEE!
THPP
THP
THIP
THIP
THIP

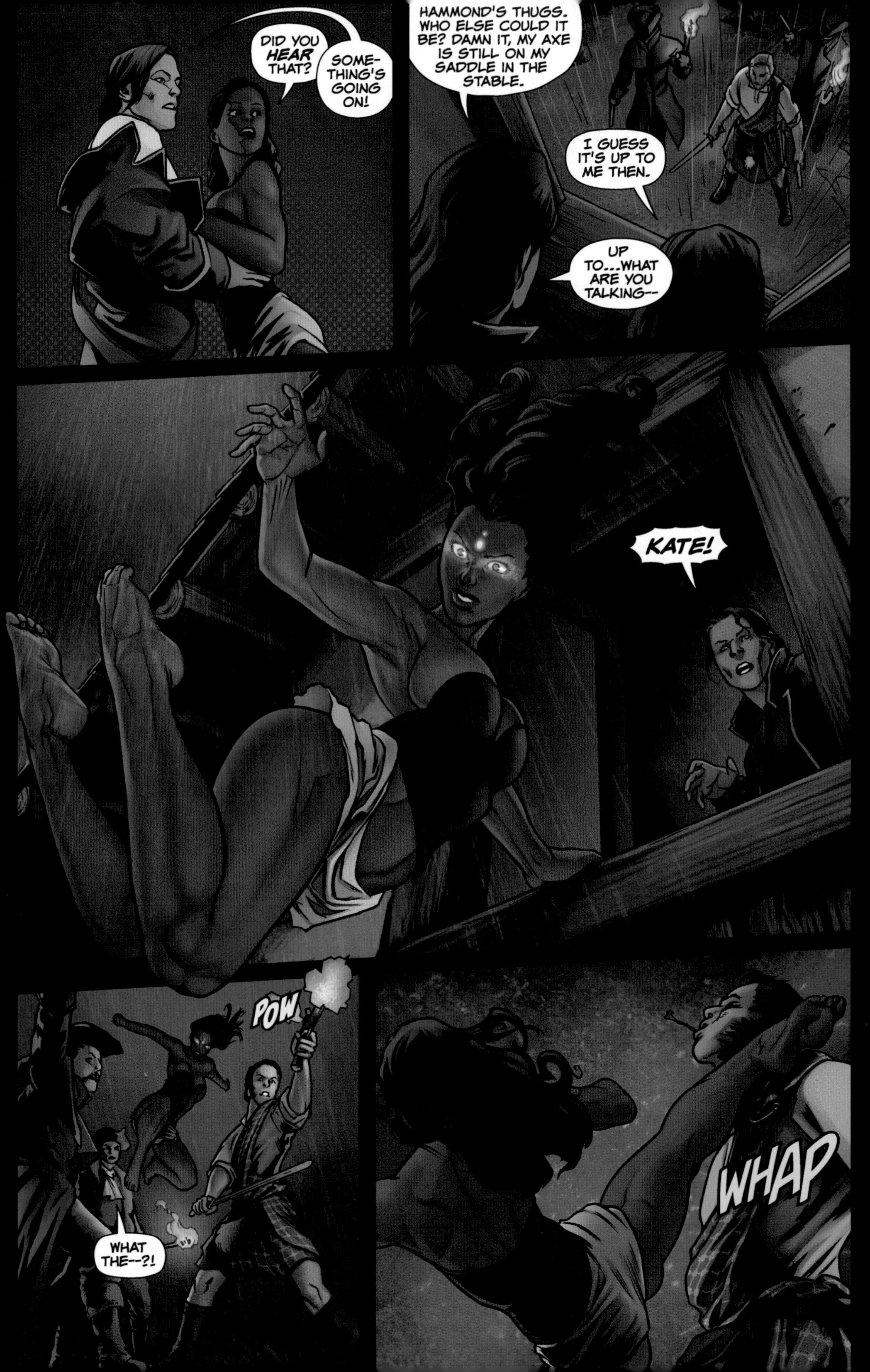
DID YOU HEAR THAT?
SOME-THING'S GOING ON!
HAMMOND'S THUGS. WHO ELSE COULD IT BE? DAMN IT, MY AXE IS STILL ON MY SADDLE IN THE STABLE.
I GUESS IT'S UP TO ME THEN.
UP TO...WHAT ARE YOU TALKING--
KATE!
POW
WHAT THE--?!
WHAP

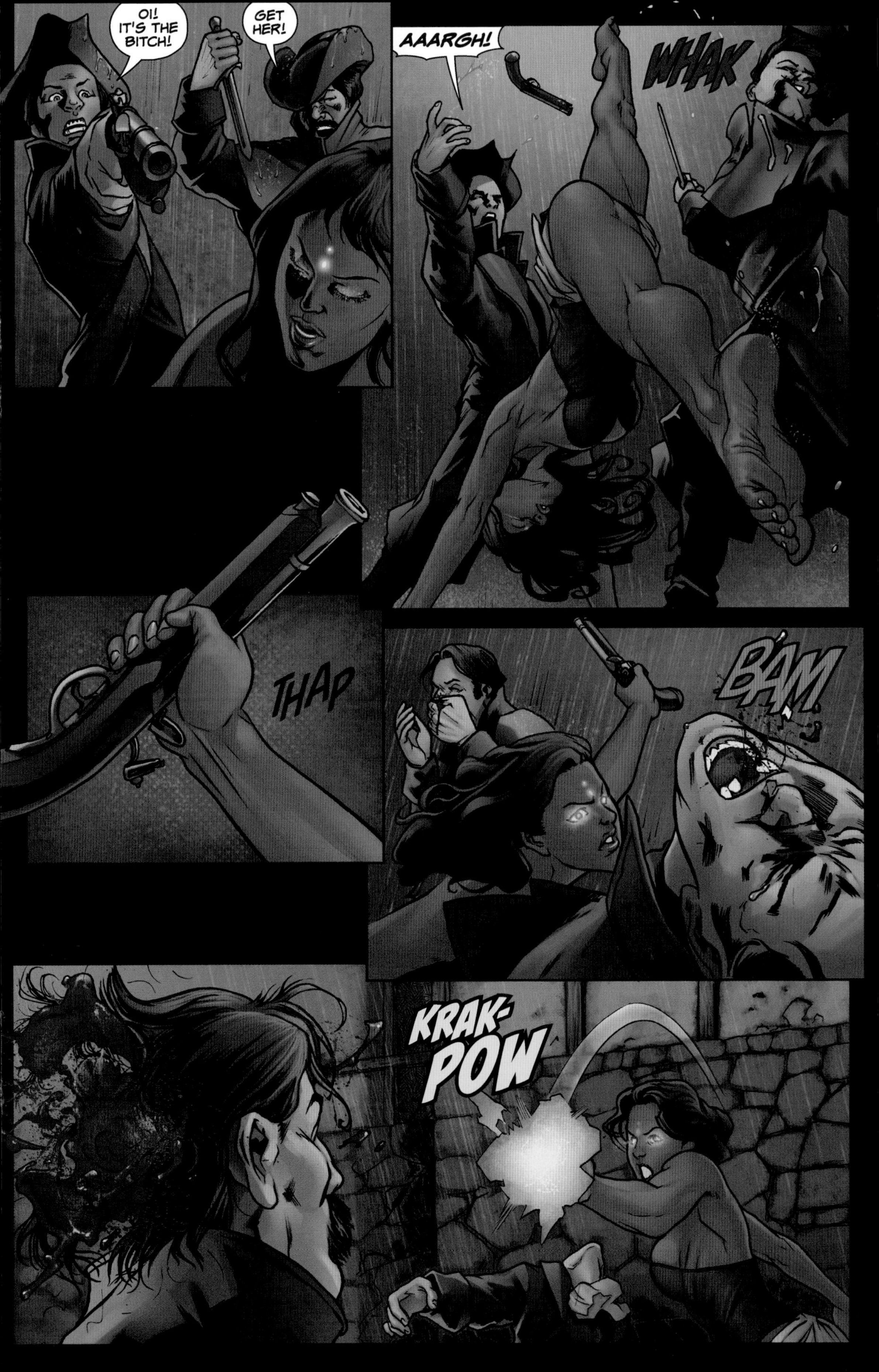
OI! IT'S THE BITCH!
GET HER!
AAARGH!
WHAK
THAP
BAM!
KRAK-POW

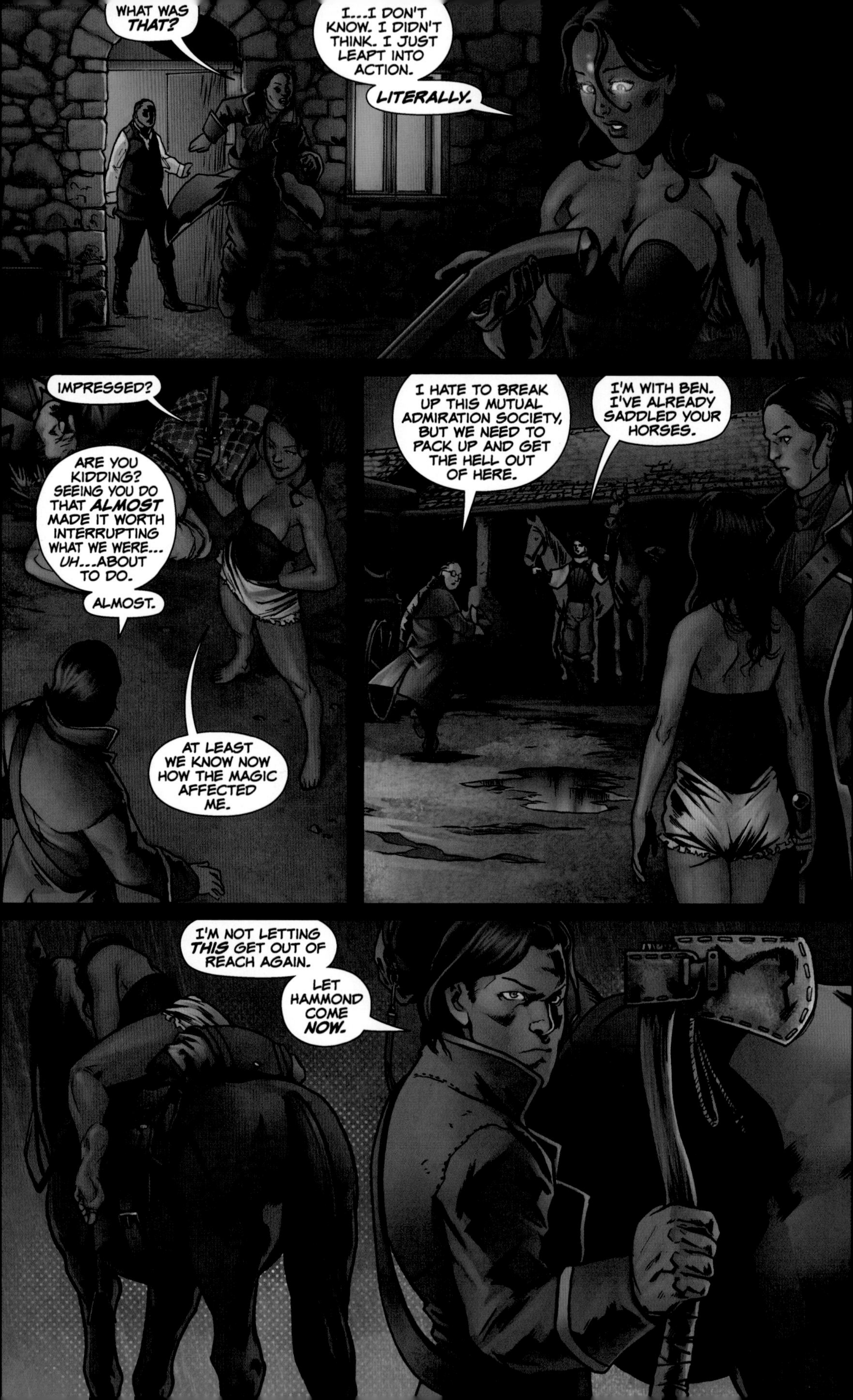
WHAT WAS THAT?
I...I DON'T KNOW. I DIDN'T THINK. I JUST LEAPT INTO ACTION.
LITERALLY.
IMPRESSED?
ARE YOU KIDDING? SEEING YOU DO THAT ALMOST MADE IT WORTH INTERRUPTING WHAT WE WERE... UH...ABOUT TO DO.
ALMOST.
AT LEAST WE KNOW NOW HOW THE MAGIC AFFECTED ME.
I HATE TO BREAK UP THIS MUTUAL ADMIRATION SOCIETY, BUT WE NEED TO PACK UP AND GET THE HELL OUT OF HERE.
I'M WITH BEN. I'VE ALREADY SADDLED YOUR HORSES.
I'M NOT LETTING THIS GET OUT OF REACH AGAIN.
LET HAMMOND COME NOW.

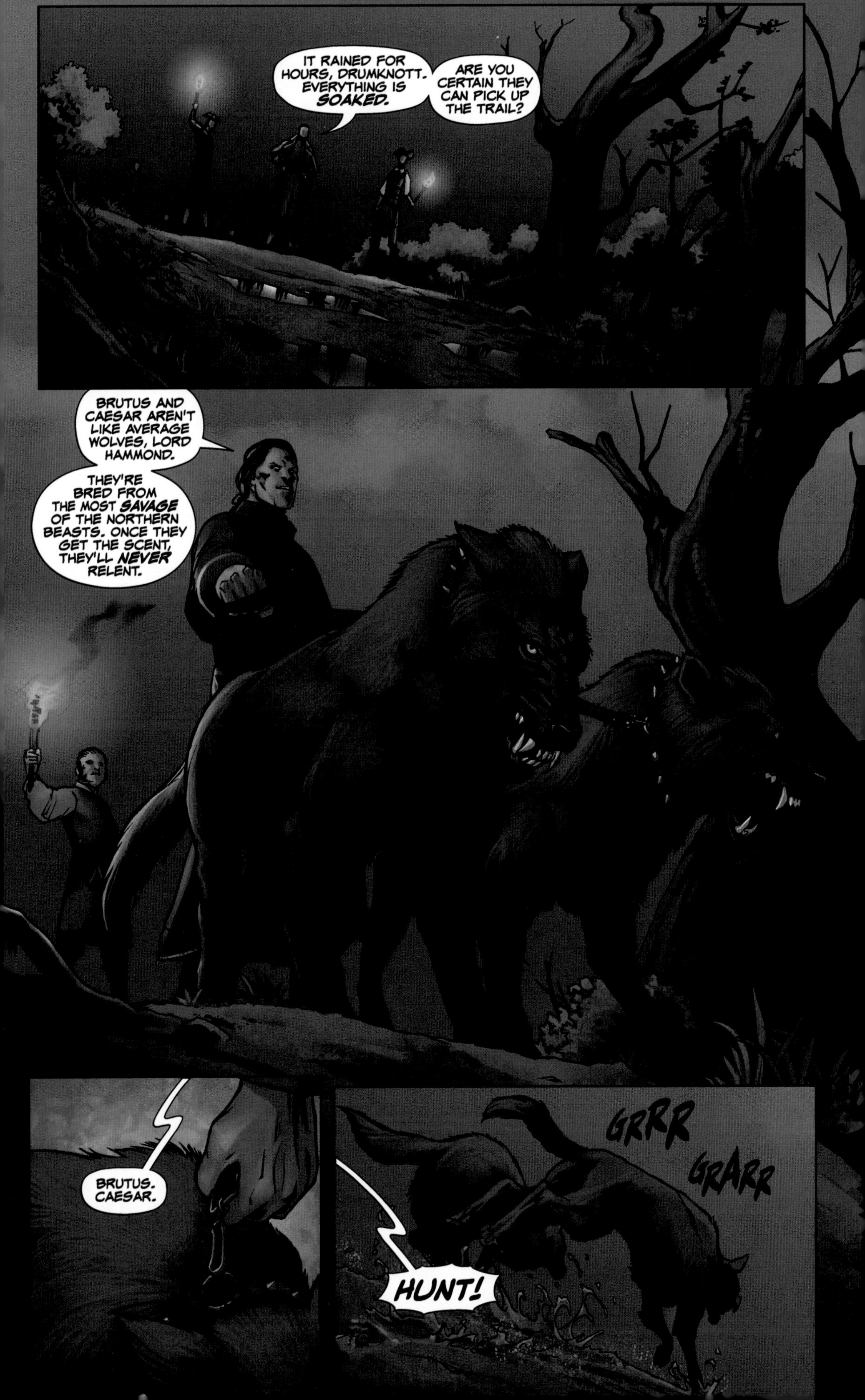
IT RAINED FOR HOURS, DRUMKNOTT. EVERYTHING IS SOAKED.
ARE YOU CERTAIN THEY CAN PICK UP THE TRAIL?
BRUTUS AND CAESAR AREN'T LIKE AVERAGE WOLVES, LORD HAMMOND.
THEY'RE BRED FROM THE MOST SAVAGE OF THE NORTHERN BEASTS. ONCE THEY GET THE SCENT, THEY'LL NEVER RELENT.
BRUTUS. CAESAR.
HUNT!
GRRR
GRARR

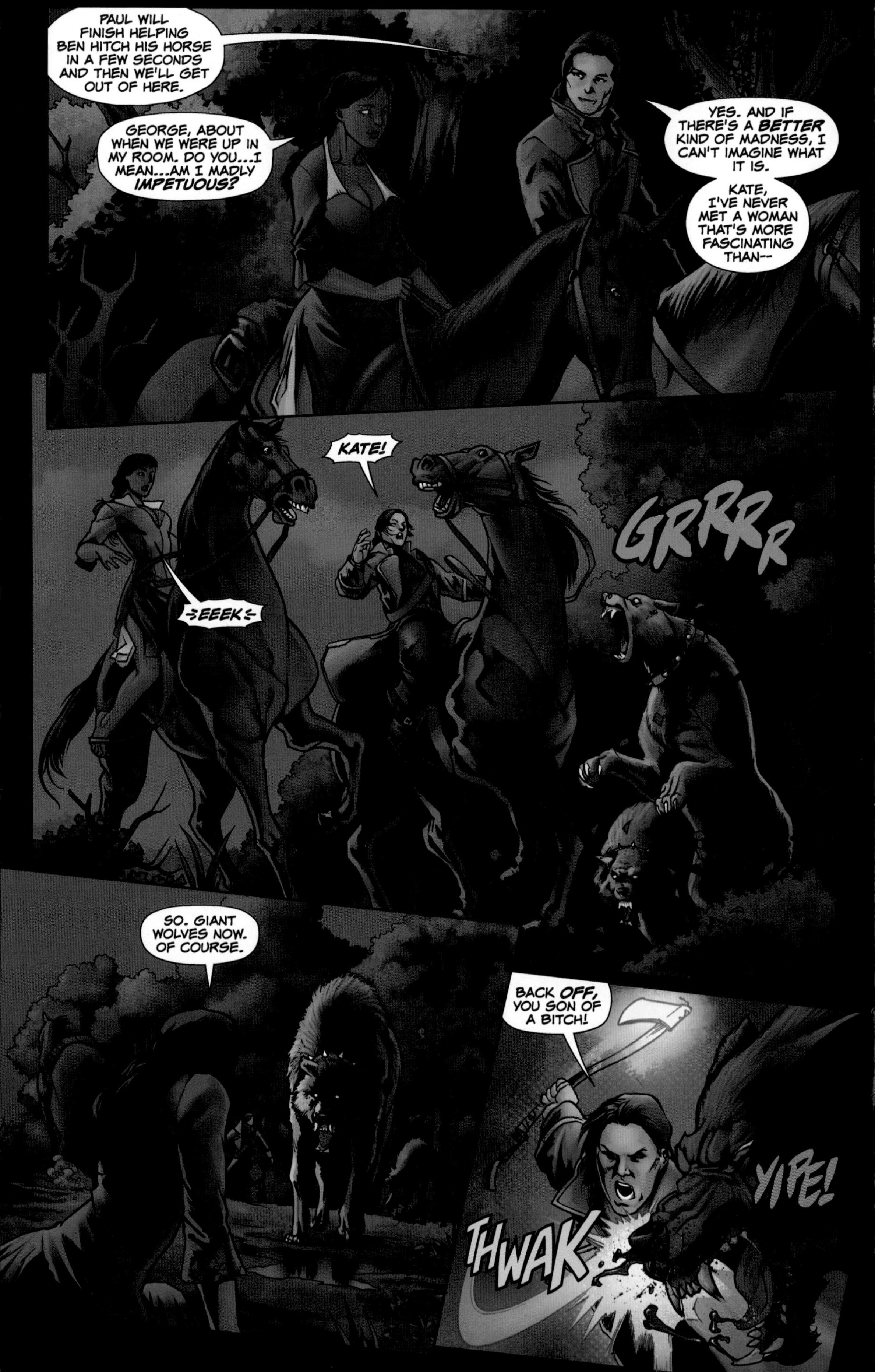
PAUL WILL FINISH HELPING BEN HITCH HIS HORSE IN A FEW SECONDS AND THEN WE'LL GET OUT OF HERE.
GEORGE, ABOUT WHEN WE WERE UP IN MY ROOM. DO YOU...I MEAN...AM I MADLY IMPETUOUS?
YES. AND IF THERE'S A BETTER KIND OF MADNESS, I CAN'T IMAGINE WHAT IT IS.
KATE, I'VE NEVER MET A WOMAN THAT'S MORE FASCINATING THAN--
KATE!
EEEK
GRRRR
SO. GIANT WOLVES NOW. OF COURSE.
BACK OFF, YOU SON OF A BITCH!
YIPE!
THWAK

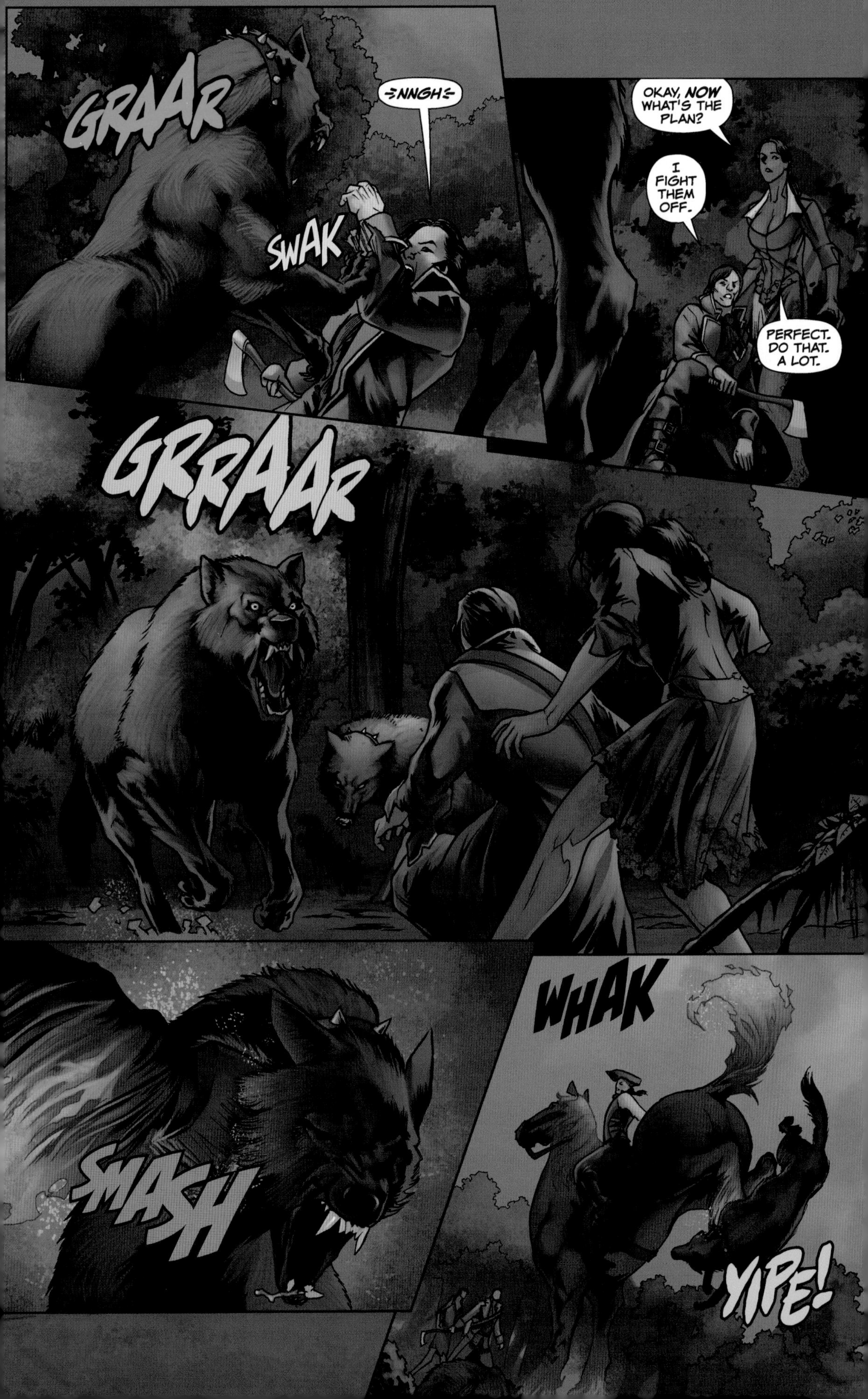
GRAAR
-NNGH-
SWAK
OKAY, NOW WHAT'S THE PLAN?
I FIGHT THEM OFF.
PERFECT. DO THAT. A LOT.
GRRAAR
SMASH
WHAK
YIPE!

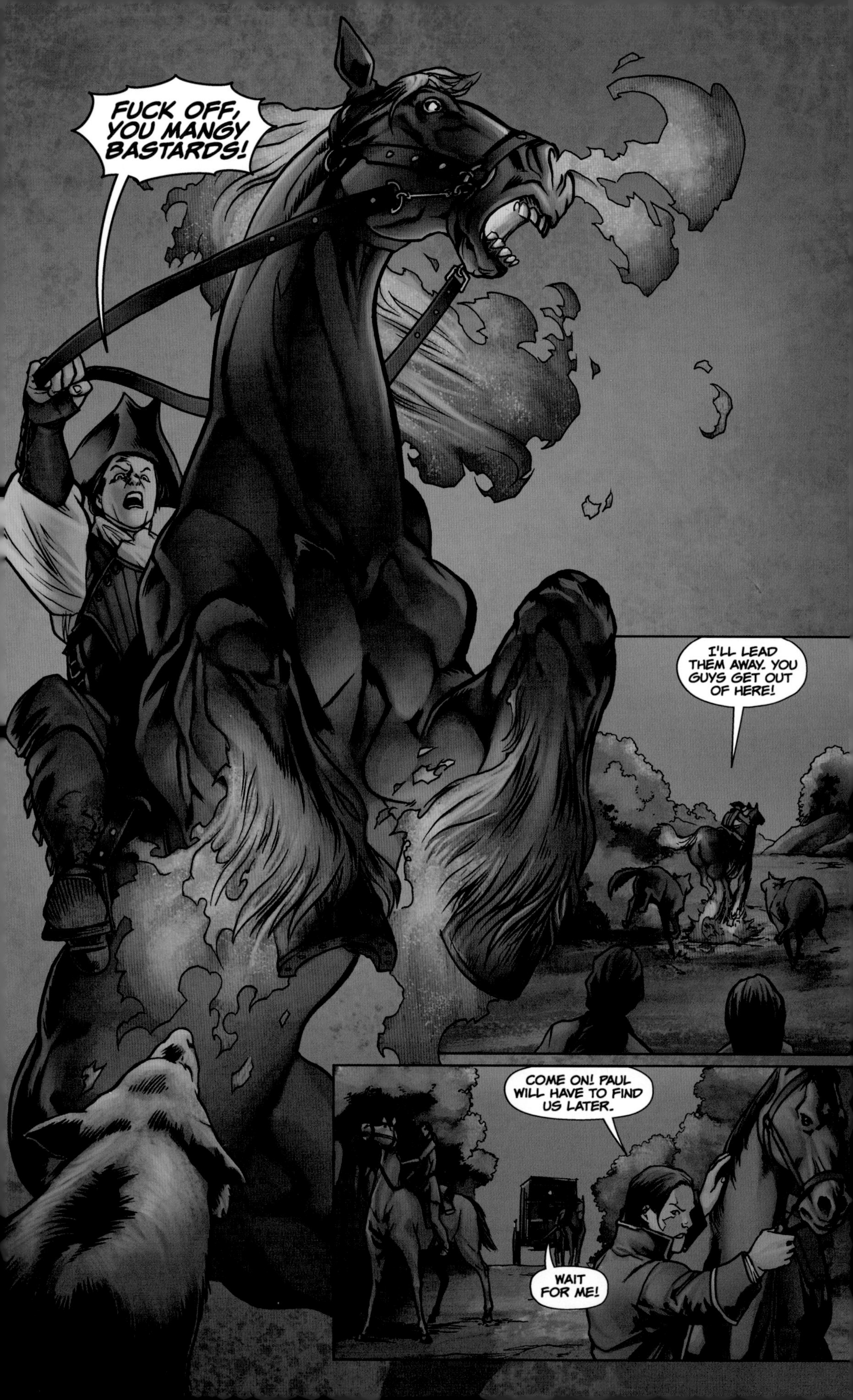
FUCK OFF, YOU MANGY BASTARDS!
I'LL LEAD THEM AWAY. YOU GUYS GET OUT OF HERE!
COME ON! PAUL WILL HAVE TO FIND US LATER.
WAIT FOR ME!

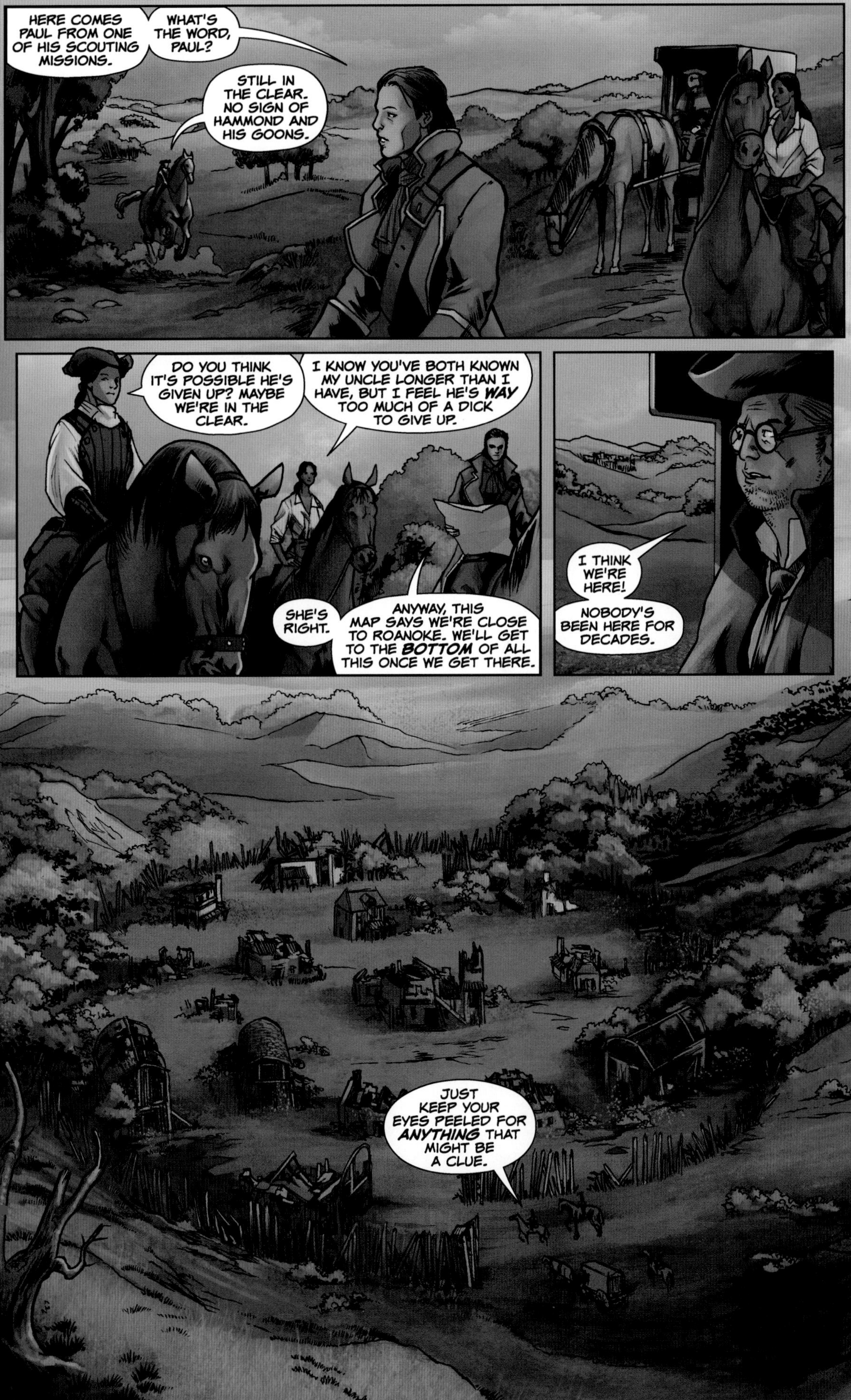
HERE COMES PAUL FROM ONE OF HIS SCOUTING MISSIONS.
WHAT'S THE WORD, PAUL?
STILL IN THE CLEAR. NO SIGN OF HAMMOND AND HIS GOONS.
DO YOU THINK IT'S POSSIBLE HE'S GIVEN UP? MAYBE WE'RE IN THE CLEAR.
I KNOW YOU'VE BOTH KNOWN MY UNCLE LONGER THAN I HAVE, BUT I FEEL HE'S WAY TOO MUCH OF A DICK TO GIVE UP.
SHE'S RIGHT.
ANYWAY, THIS MAP SAYS WE'RE CLOSE TO ROANOKE. WE'LL GET TO THE BOTTOM OF ALL THIS ONCE WE GET THERE.
I THINK WE'RE HERE!
NOBODY'S BEEN HERE FOR DECADES.
JUST KEEP YOUR EYES PEELED FOR ANYTHING THAT MIGHT BE A CLUE.

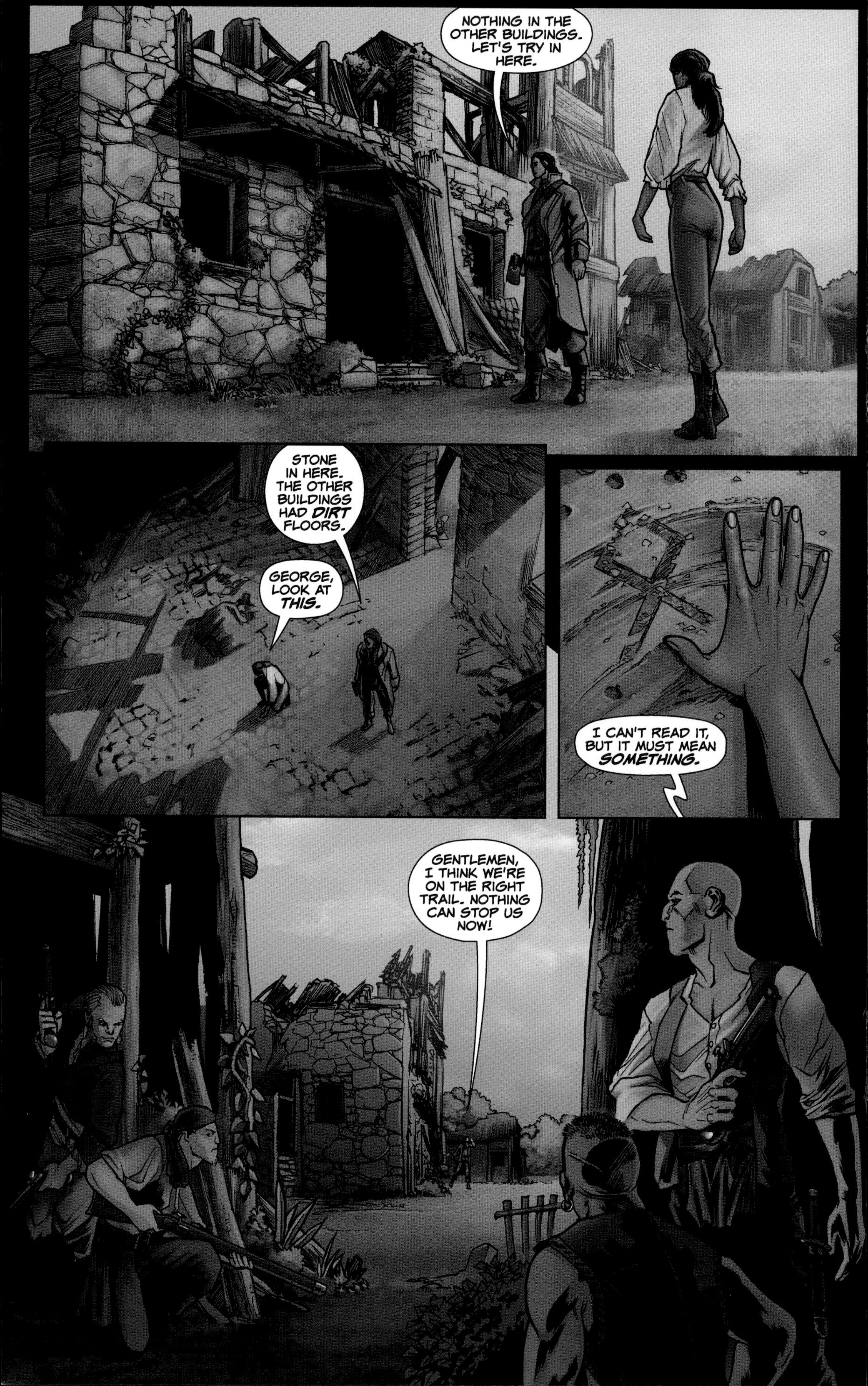
NOTHING IN THE OTHER BUILDINGS. LET'S TRY IN HERE.
STONE IN HERE. THE OTHER BUILDINGS HAD DIRT FLOORS.
GEORGE, LOOK AT THIS.
I CAN'T READ IT, BUT IT MUST MEAN SOMETHING.
GENTLEMEN, I THINK WE'RE ON THE RIGHT TRAIL. NOTHING CAN STOP US NOW!

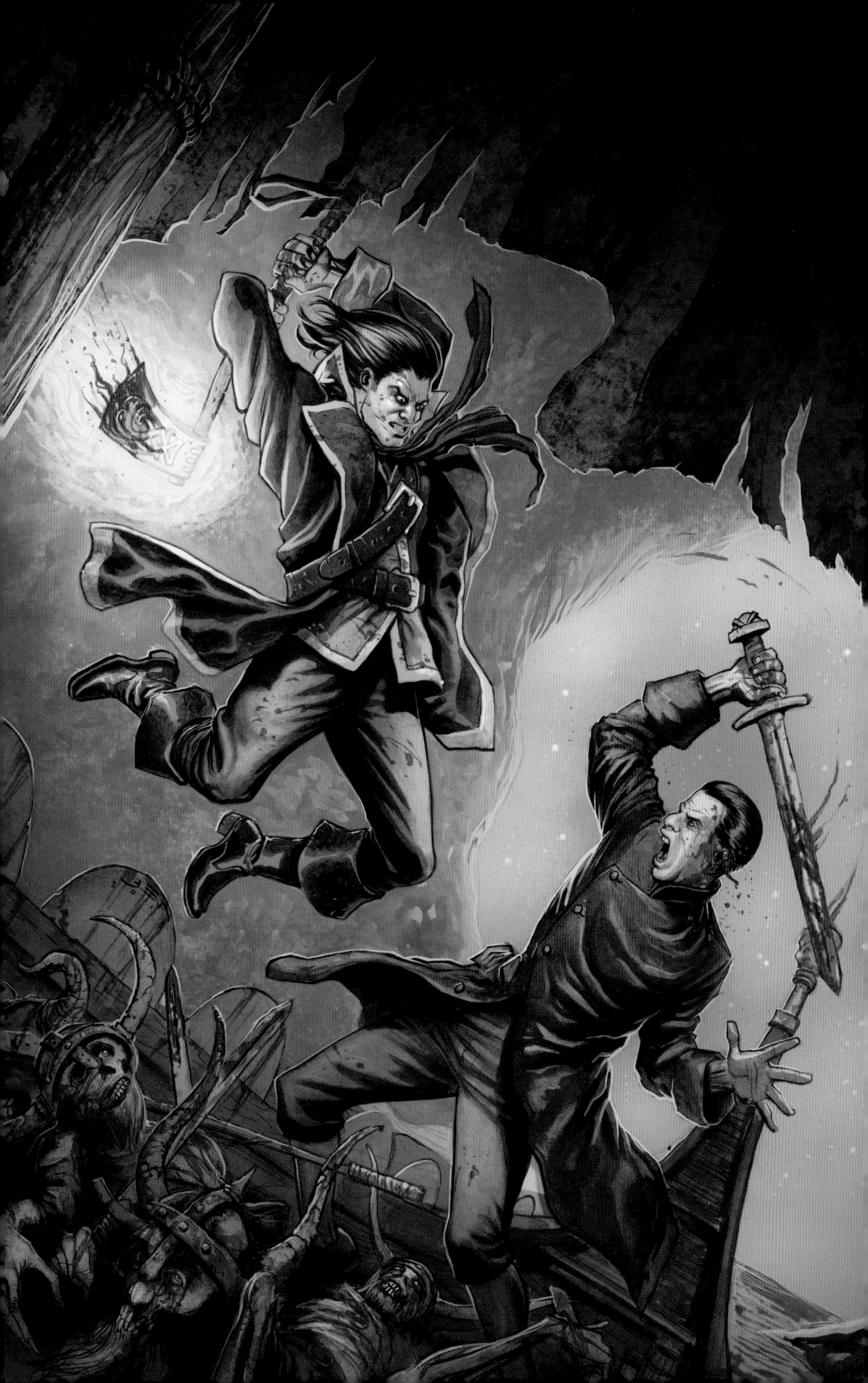

III

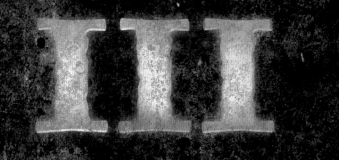

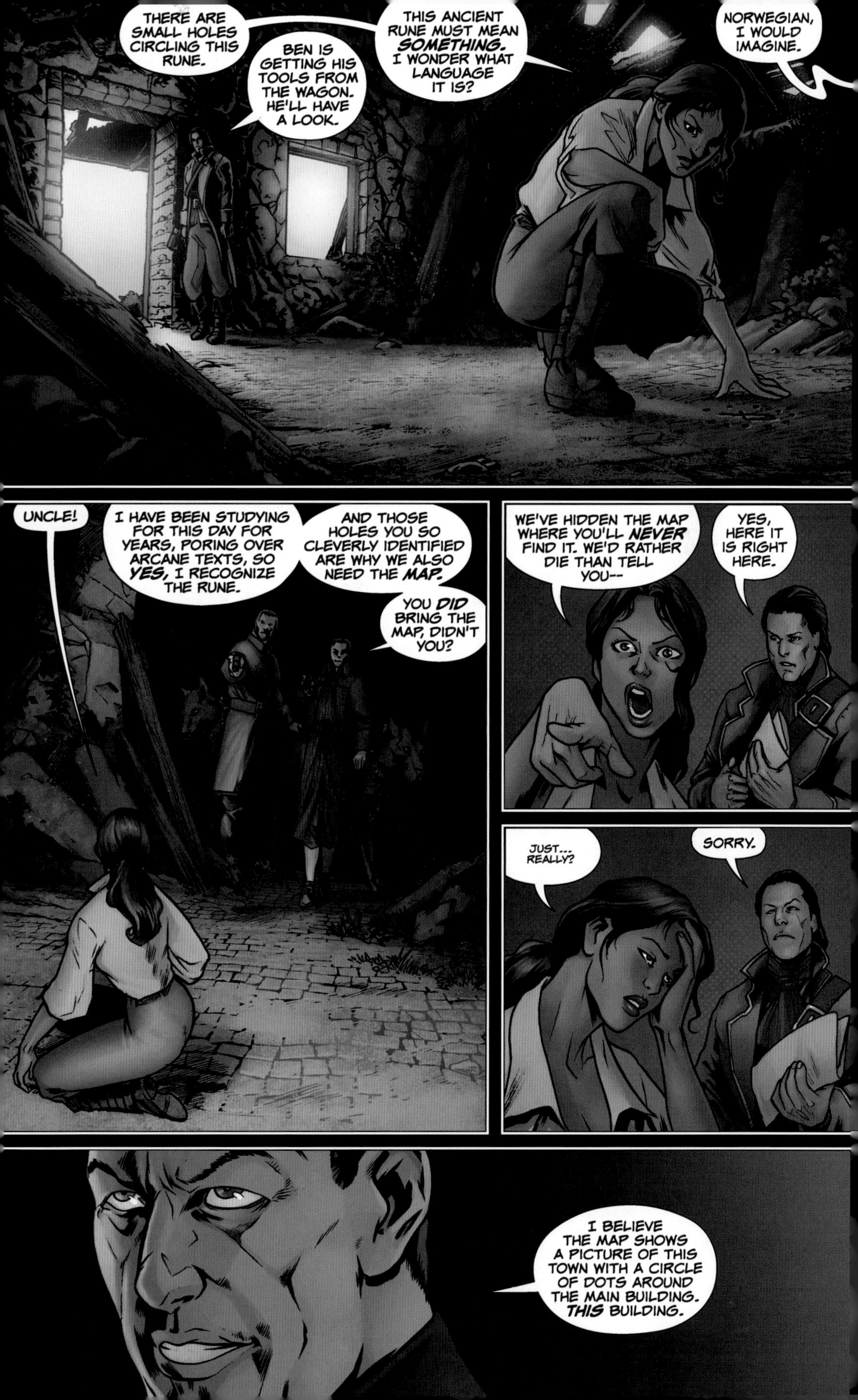
THERE ARE SMALL HOLES CIRCLING THIS RUNE.
THIS ANCIENT RUNE MUST MEAN SOMETHING. I WONDER WHAT LANGUAGE IT IS?
BEN IS GETTING HIS TOOLS FROM THE WAGON. HE'LL HAVE A LOOK.
NORWEGIAN, I WOULD IMAGINE.
UNCLE!
I HAVE BEEN STUDYING FOR THIS DAY FOR YEARS, PORING OVER ARCANE TEXTS, SO YES, I RECOGNIZE THE RUNE.
AND THOSE HOLES YOU SO CLEVERLY IDENTIFIED ARE WHY WE ALSO NEED THE MAP.
YOU DID BRING THE MAP, DIDN'T YOU?
WE'VE HIDDEN THE MAP WHERE YOU'LL NEVER FIND IT. WE'D RATHER DIE THAN TELL YOU--
YES, HERE IT IS RIGHT HERE.
JUST... REALLY?
SORRY.
I BELIEVE THE MAP SHOWS A PICTURE OF THIS TOWN WITH A CIRCLE OF DOTS AROUND THE MAIN BUILDING. THIS BUILDING.

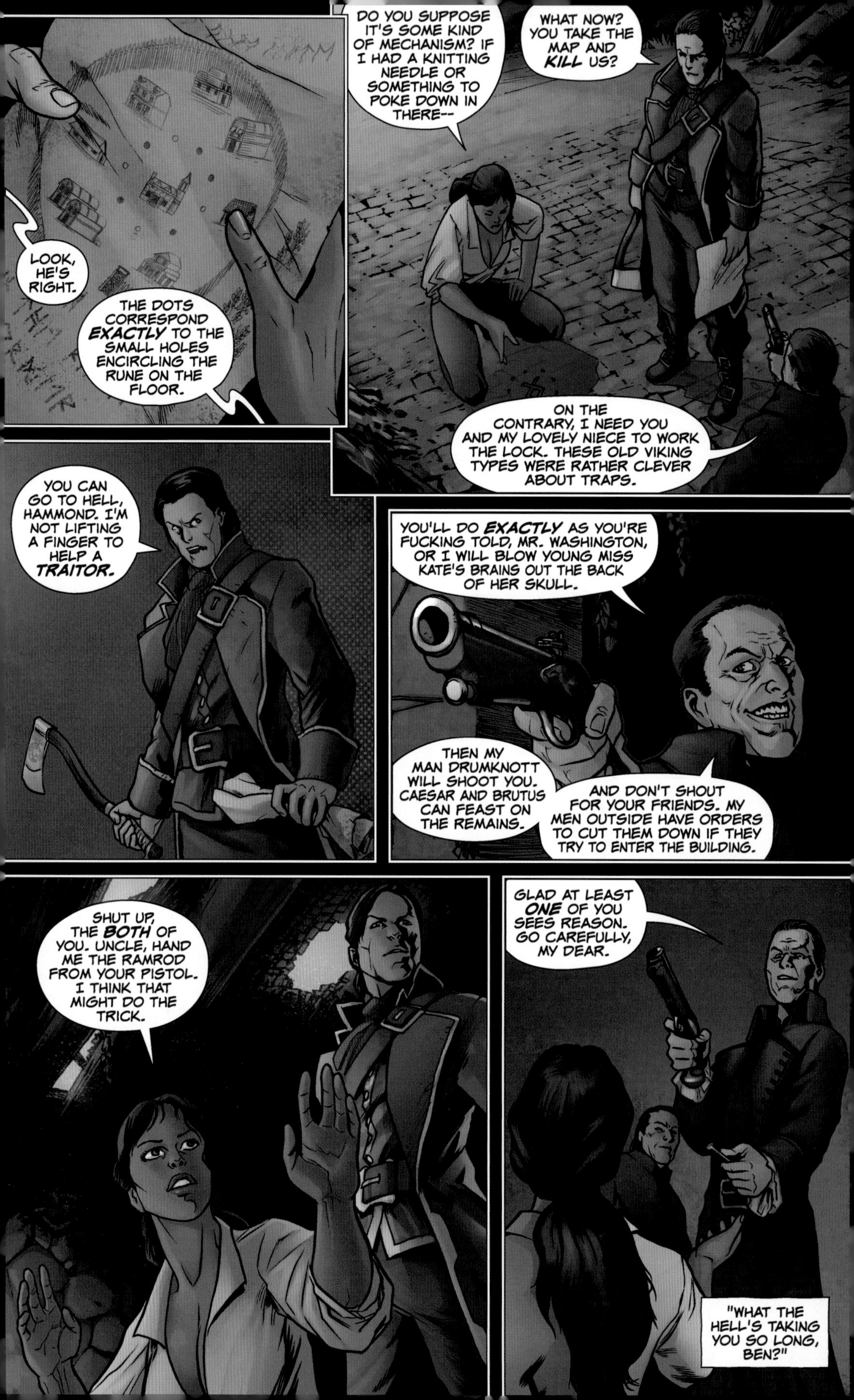
LOOK, HE'S RIGHT.
THE DOTS CORRESPOND EXACTLY TO THE SMALL HOLES ENCIRCLING THE RUNE ON THE FLOOR.
DO YOU SUPPOSE IT'S SOME KIND OF MECHANISM? IF I HAD A KNITTING NEEDLE OR SOMETHING TO POKE DOWN IN THERE--
WHAT NOW? YOU TAKE THE MAP AND KILL US?
ON THE CONTRARY, I NEED YOU AND MY LOVELY NIECE TO WORK THE LOCK. THESE OLD VIKING TYPES WERE RATHER CLEVER ABOUT TRAPS.
YOU CAN GO TO HELL, HAMMOND. I'M NOT LIFTING A FINGER TO HELP A TRAITOR.
YOU'LL DO EXACTLY AS YOU'RE FUCKING TOLD, MR. WASHINGTON, OR I WILL BLOW YOUNG MISS KATE'S BRAINS OUT THE BACK OF HER SKULL.
THEN MY MAN DRUMKNOTT WILL SHOOT YOU. CAESAR AND BRUTUS CAN FEAST ON THE REMAINS.
AND DON'T SHOUT FOR YOUR FRIENDS. MY MEN OUTSIDE HAVE ORDERS TO CUT THEM DOWN IF THEY TRY TO ENTER THE BUILDING.
SHUT UP, THE BOTH OF YOU. UNCLE, HAND ME THE RAMROD FROM YOUR PISTOL. I THINK THAT MIGHT DO THE TRICK.
GLAD AT LEAST ONE OF YOU SEES REASON. GO CAREFULLY, MY DEAR.
"WHAT THE HELL'S TAKING YOU SO LONG, BEN?"

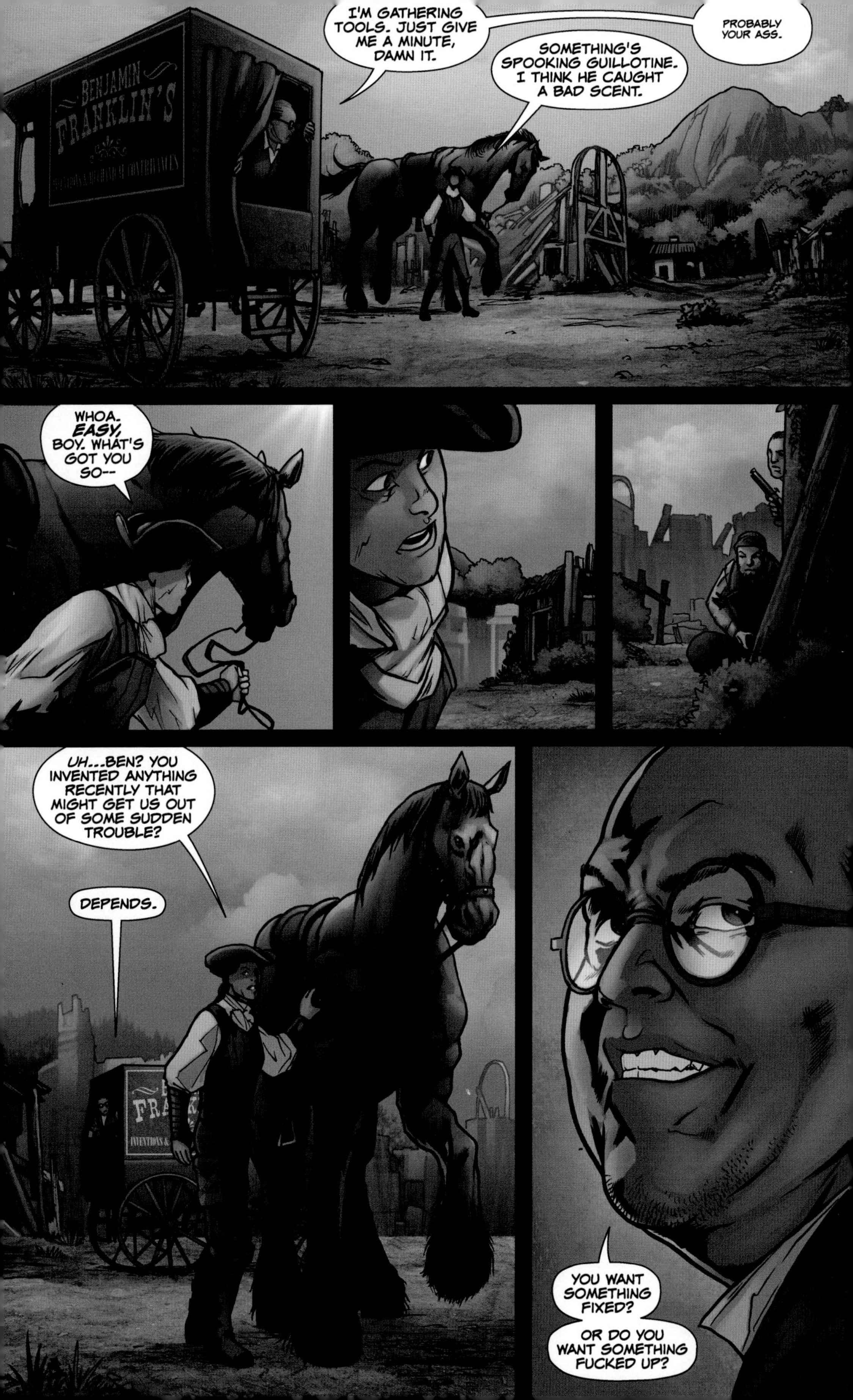
BENJAMIN FRANKLIN'S
I'M GATHERING TOOLS. JUST GIVE ME A MINUTE, DAMN IT.
SOMETHING'S SPOOKING GUILLOTINE. I THINK HE CAUGHT A BAD SCENT.
PROBABLY YOUR ASS.
WHOA. *EASY,* BOY. WHAT'S GOT YOU SO--
UH...BEN? YOU INVENTED ANYTHING RECENTLY THAT MIGHT GET US OUT OF SOME SUDDEN TROUBLE?
DEPENDS.
YOU WANT SOMETHING FIXED?
OR DO YOU WANT SOMETHING FUCKED UP?

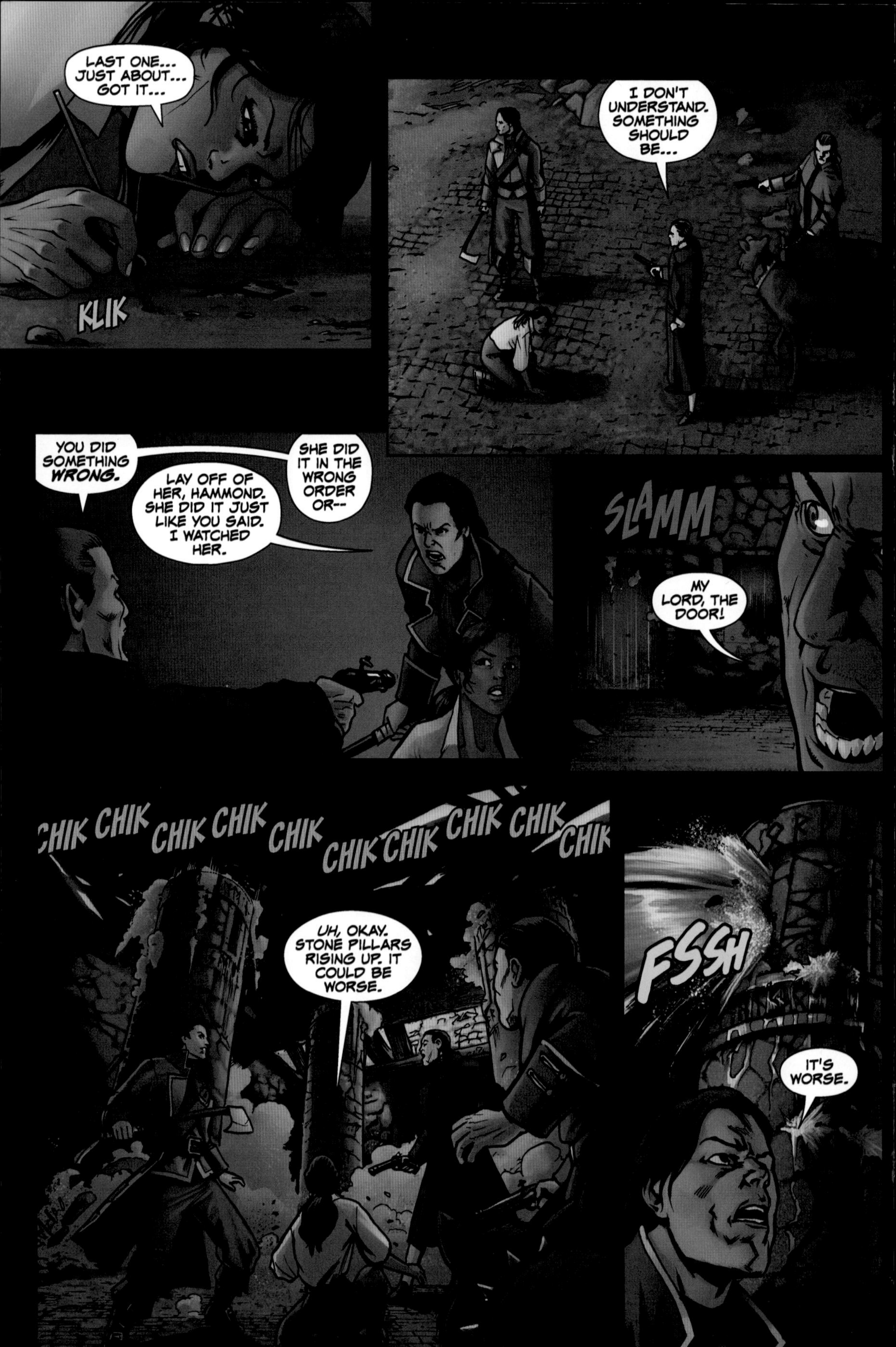
LAST ONE... JUST ABOUT... GOT IT...
KLIK
I DON'T UNDERSTAND. SOMETHING SHOULD BE...
YOU DID SOMETHING WRONG.
SHE DID IT IN THE WRONG ORDER OR--
LAY OFF OF HER, HAMMOND. SHE DID IT JUST LIKE YOU SAID. I WATCHED HER.
SLAMM
MY LORD, THE DOOR!
CHIK CHIK CHIK CHIK CHIK CHIK CHIK CHIK CHIK CHIK
UH, OKAY. STONE PILLARS RISING UP. IT COULD BE WORSE.
FSSH
IT'S WORSE.

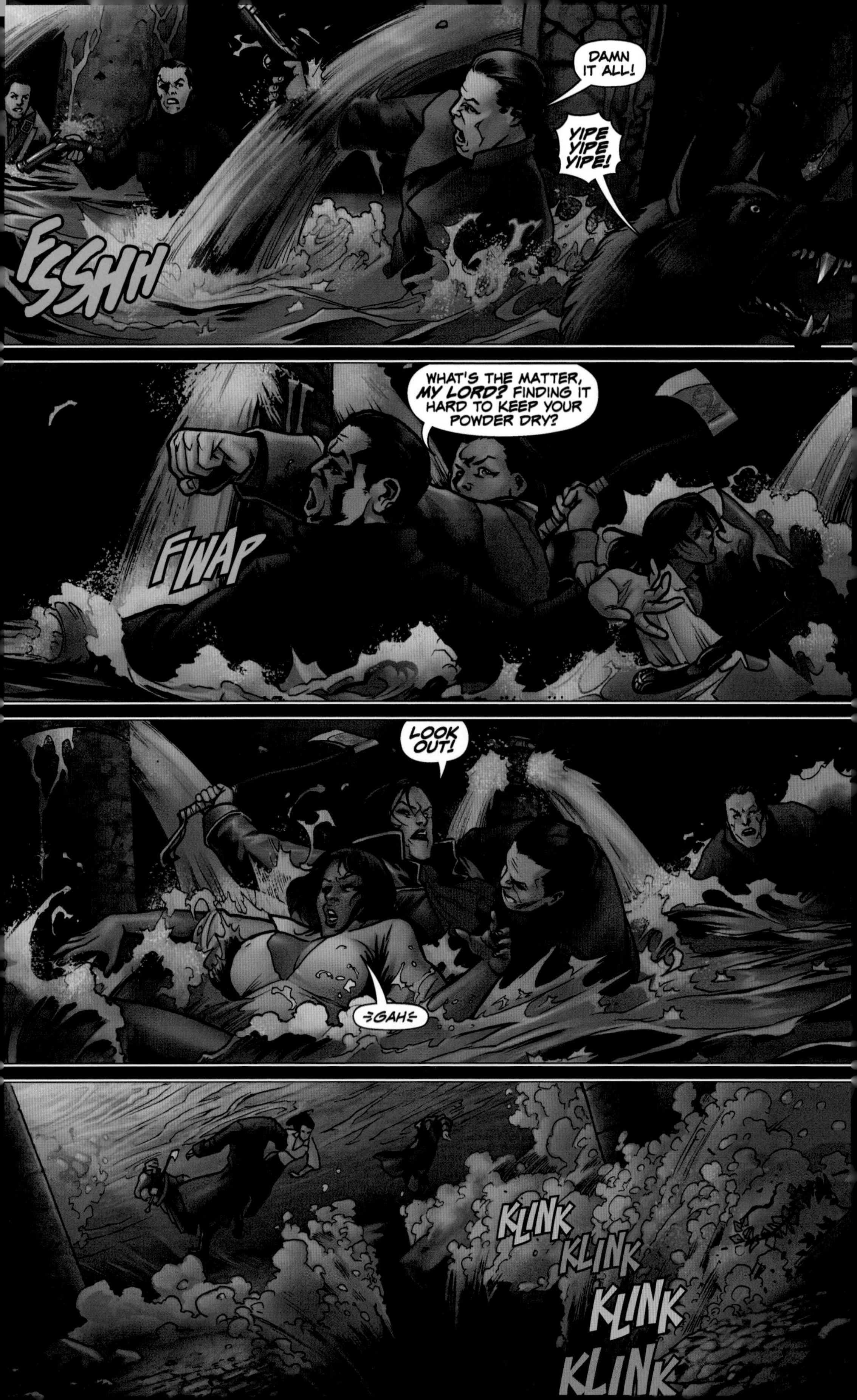
DAMN IT ALL!
YIPE YIPE YIPE!
FSSHH
WHAT'S THE MATTER, MY LORD? FINDING IT HARD TO KEEP YOUR POWDER DRY?
FWAP
LOOK OUT!
GAH
KLINK
KLINK
KLINK
KLINK

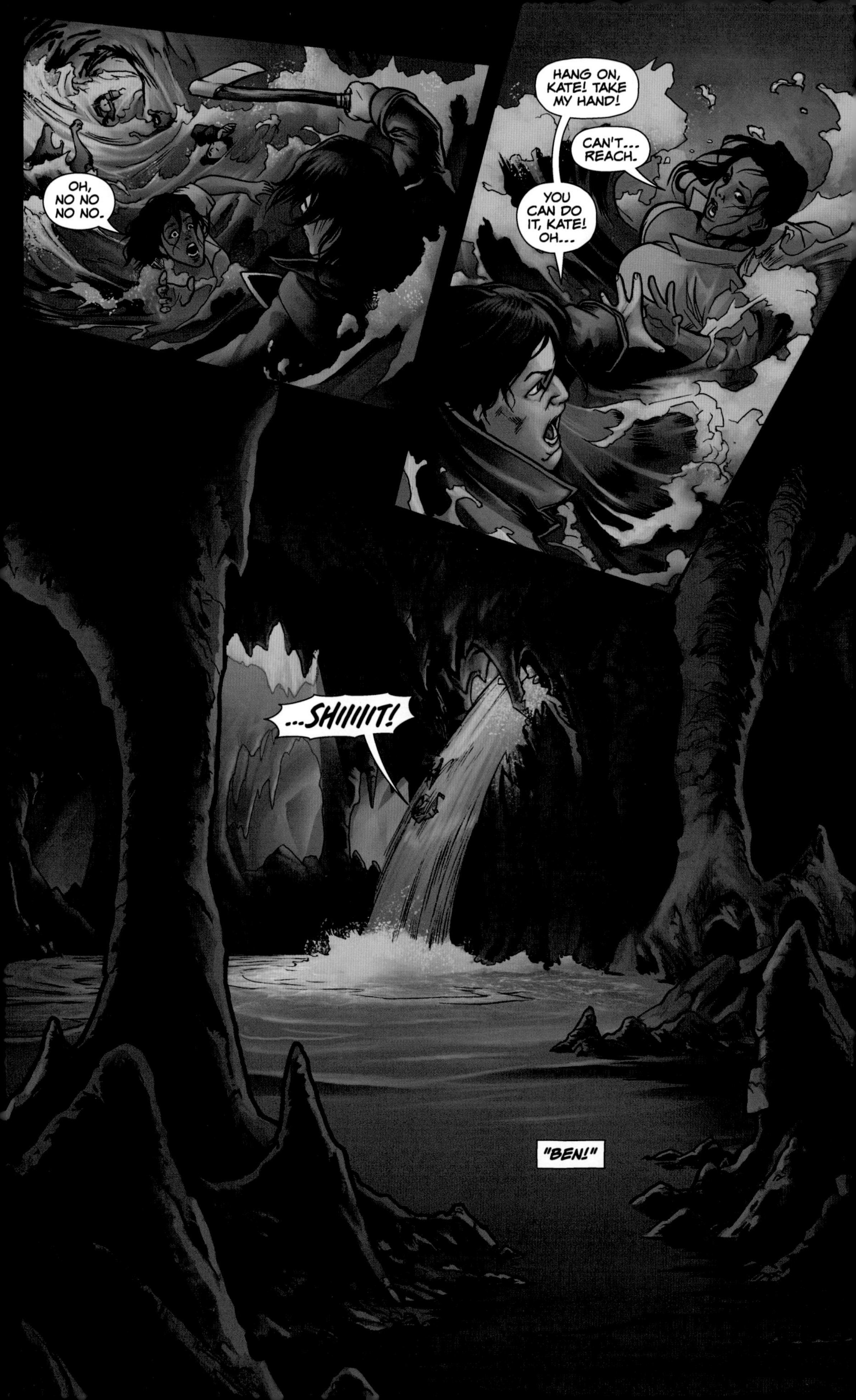
OH, NO NO NO NO.
HANG ON, KATE! TAKE MY HAND!
CAN'T... REACH.
YOU CAN DO IT, KATE! OH...
...SHIIIIIT!
"BEN!"

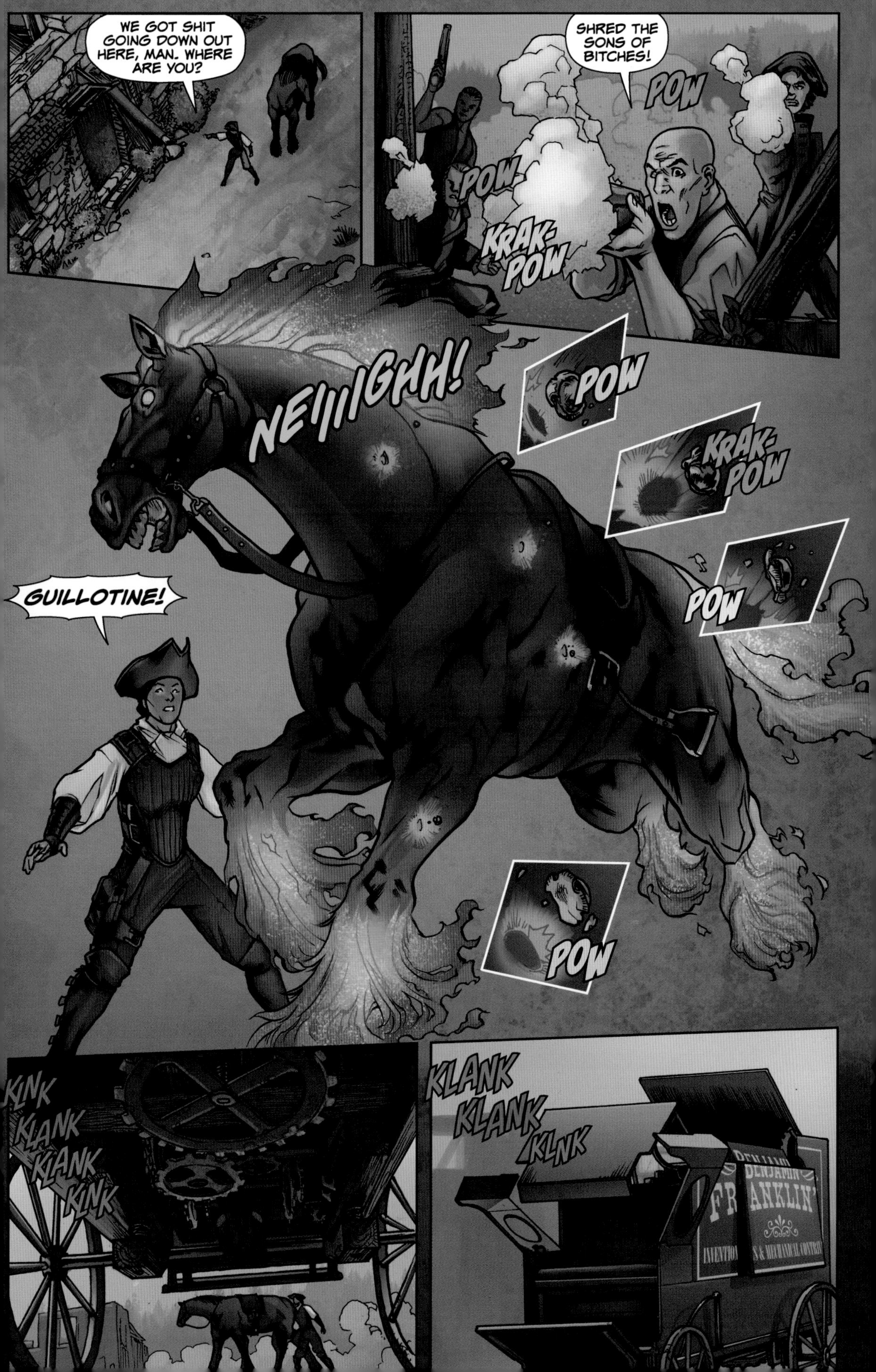
WE GOT SHIT GOING DOWN OUT HERE, MAN. WHERE ARE YOU?
SHRED THE SONS OF BITCHES!
POW
POW
KRAK-POW
NEIIIIGHH!
POW
KRAK-POW
POW
GUILLOTINE!
POW
KLNK
KLANK
KLANK
KLNK
KLANK
KLANK
KLNK
BENJAMIN FRANKLIN
INVENTIONS & MECHANICAL CONTRIV

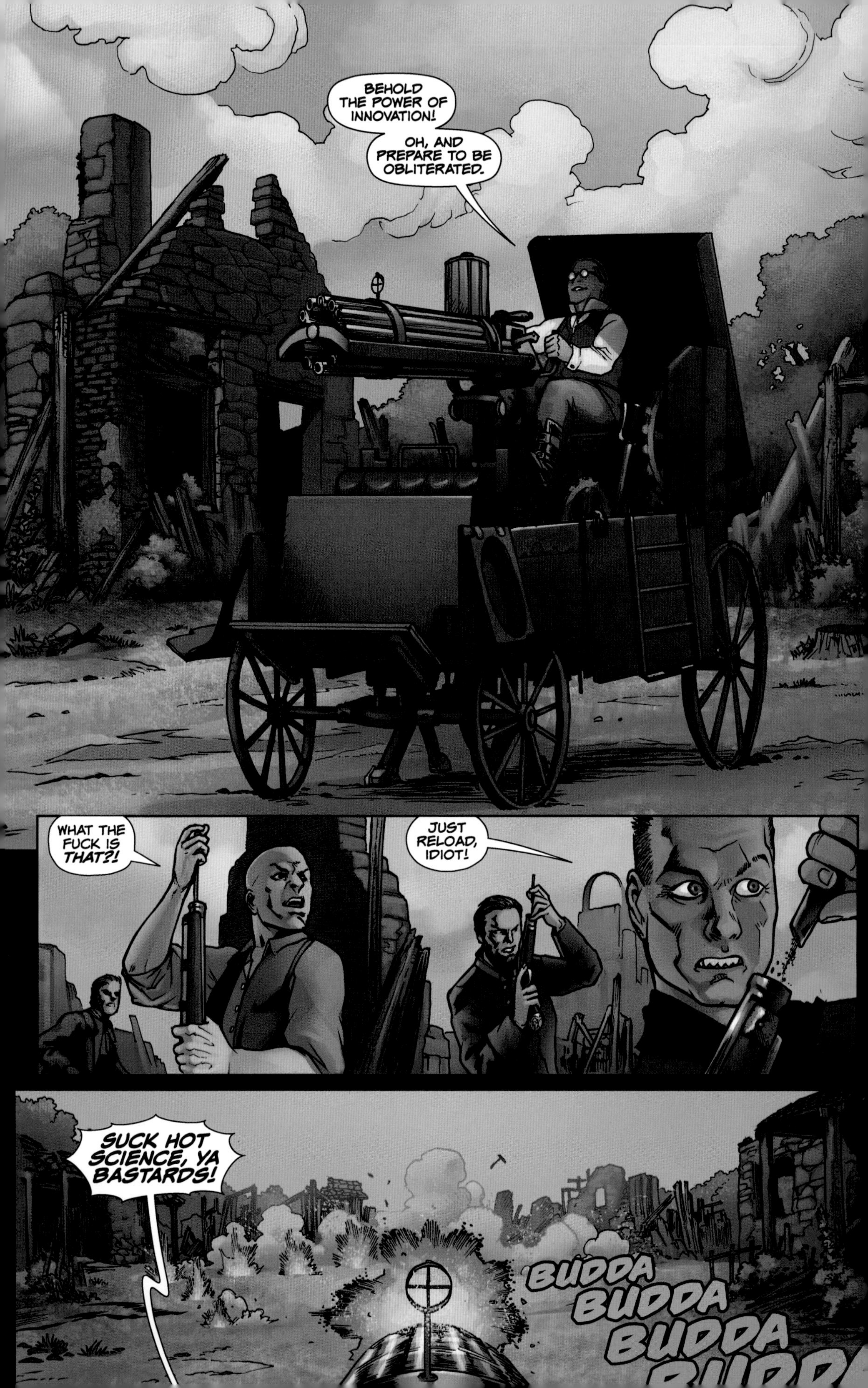
BEHOLD THE POWER OF INNOVATION!
OH, AND PREPARE TO BE OBLITERATED.
WHAT THE FUCK IS *THAT?!*
JUST RELOAD, IDIOT!
SUCK HOT SCIENCE, YA BASTARDS!
BUDDA BUDDA BUDDA

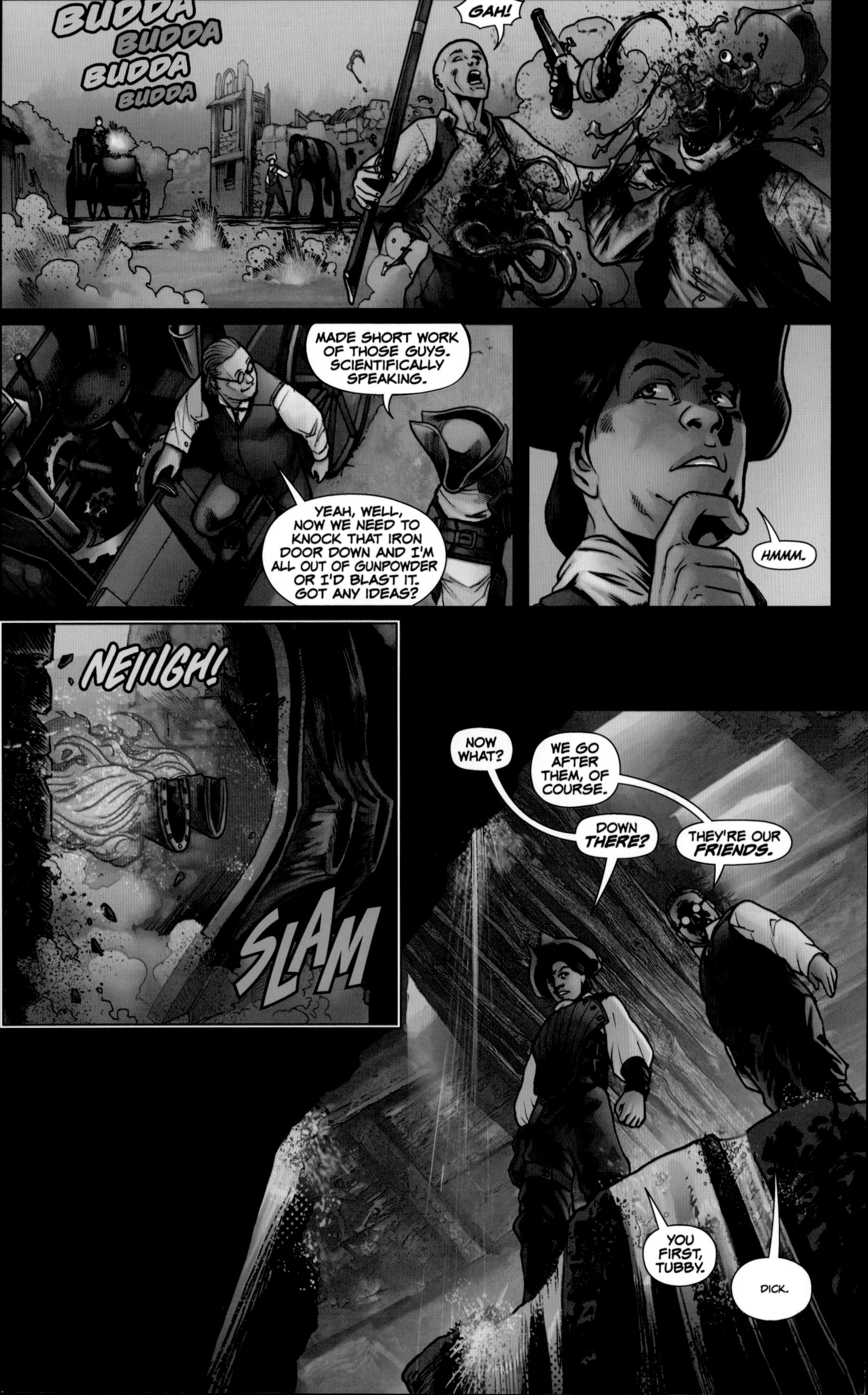
BUDDA BUDDA BUDDA BUDDA
GAH!
MADE SHORT WORK OF THOSE GUYS. SCIENTIFICALLY SPEAKING.
YEAH, WELL, NOW WE NEED TO KNOCK THAT IRON DOOR DOWN AND I'M ALL OUT OF GUNPOWDER OR I'D BLAST IT. GOT ANY IDEAS?
HMMM.
NEIIIGH!
SLAM
NOW WHAT?
WE GO AFTER THEM, OF COURSE.
DOWN THERE?
THEY'RE OUR FRIENDS.
YOU FIRST, TUBBY.
DICK.

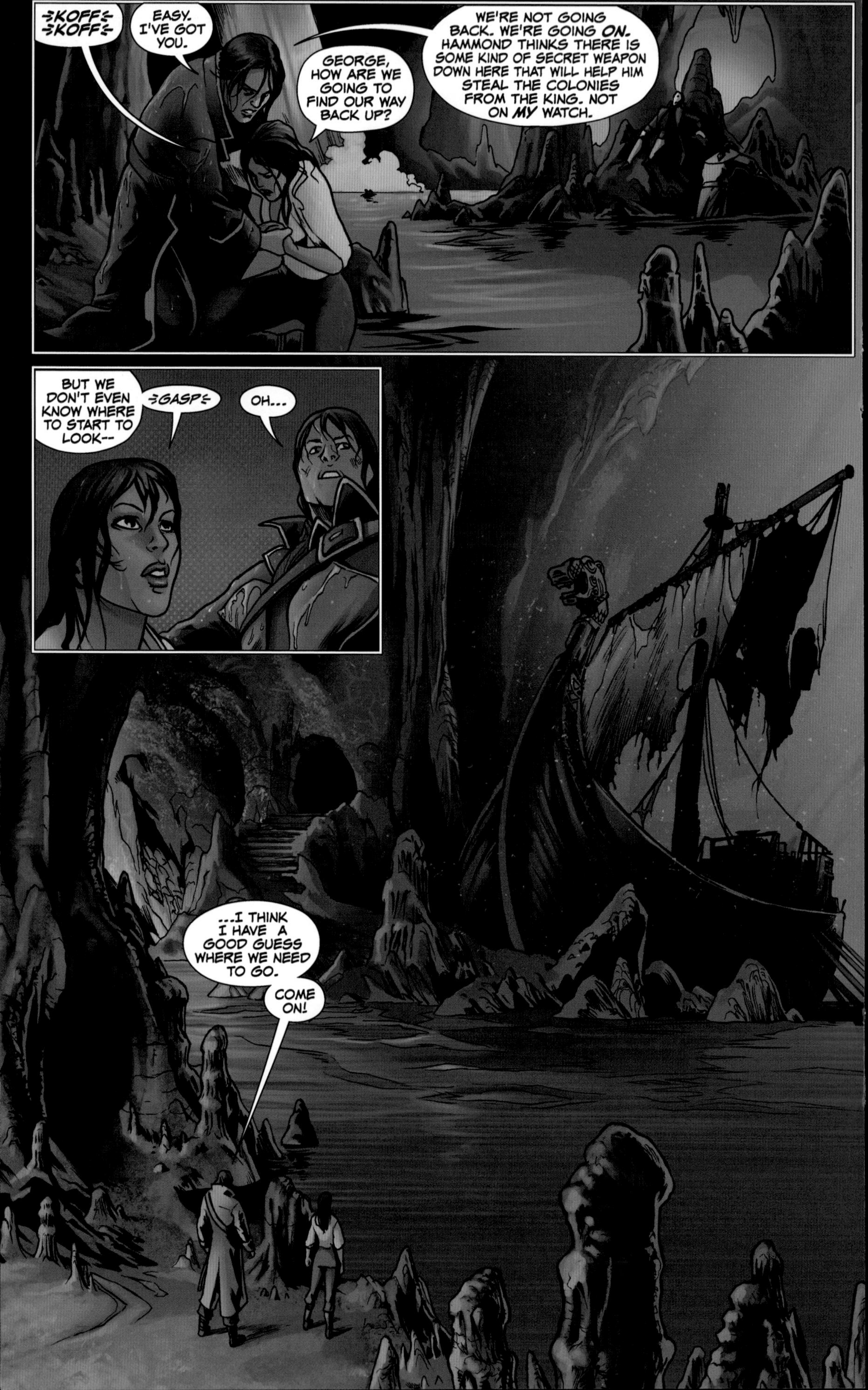
KOFF KOFF
EASY. I'VE GOT YOU.
GEORGE, HOW ARE WE GOING TO FIND OUR WAY BACK UP?
WE'RE NOT GOING BACK. WE'RE GOING ON. HAMMOND THINKS THERE IS SOME KIND OF SECRET WEAPON DOWN HERE THAT WILL HELP HIM STEAL THE COLONIES FROM THE KING. NOT ON MY WATCH.
BUT WE DON'T EVEN KNOW WHERE TO START TO LOOK--
GASP
OH...
...I THINK I HAVE A GOOD GUESS WHERE WE NEED TO GO.
COME ON!

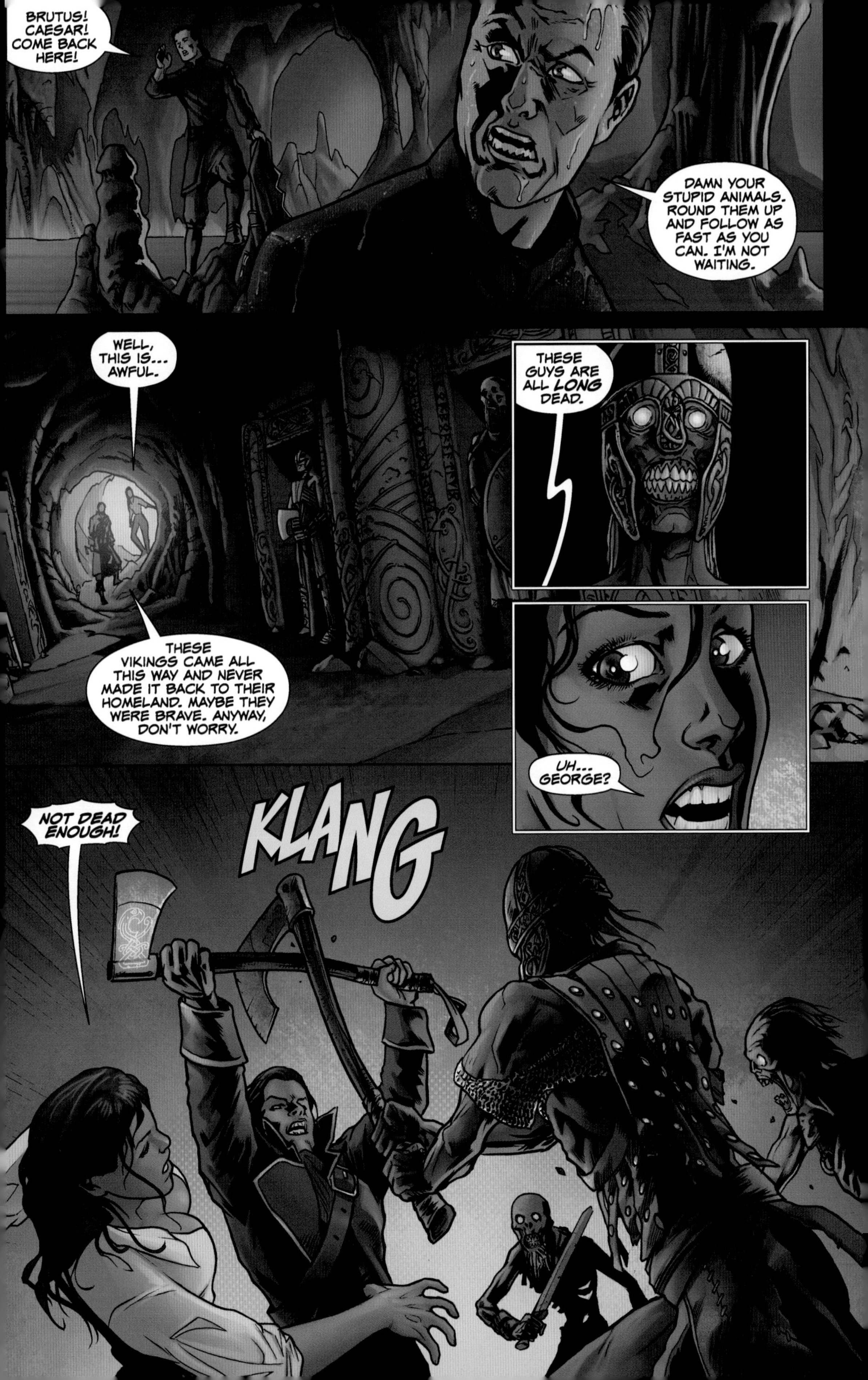
BRUTUS! CAESAR! COME BACK HERE!
DAMN YOUR STUPID ANIMALS. ROUND THEM UP AND FOLLOW AS FAST AS YOU CAN. I'M NOT WAITING.
WELL, THIS IS... AWFUL.
THESE VIKINGS CAME ALL THIS WAY AND NEVER MADE IT BACK TO THEIR HOMELAND. MAYBE THEY WERE BRAVE. ANYWAY, DON'T WORRY.
THESE GUYS ARE ALL LONG DEAD.
UH... GEORGE?
NOT DEAD ENOUGH!
KLANG

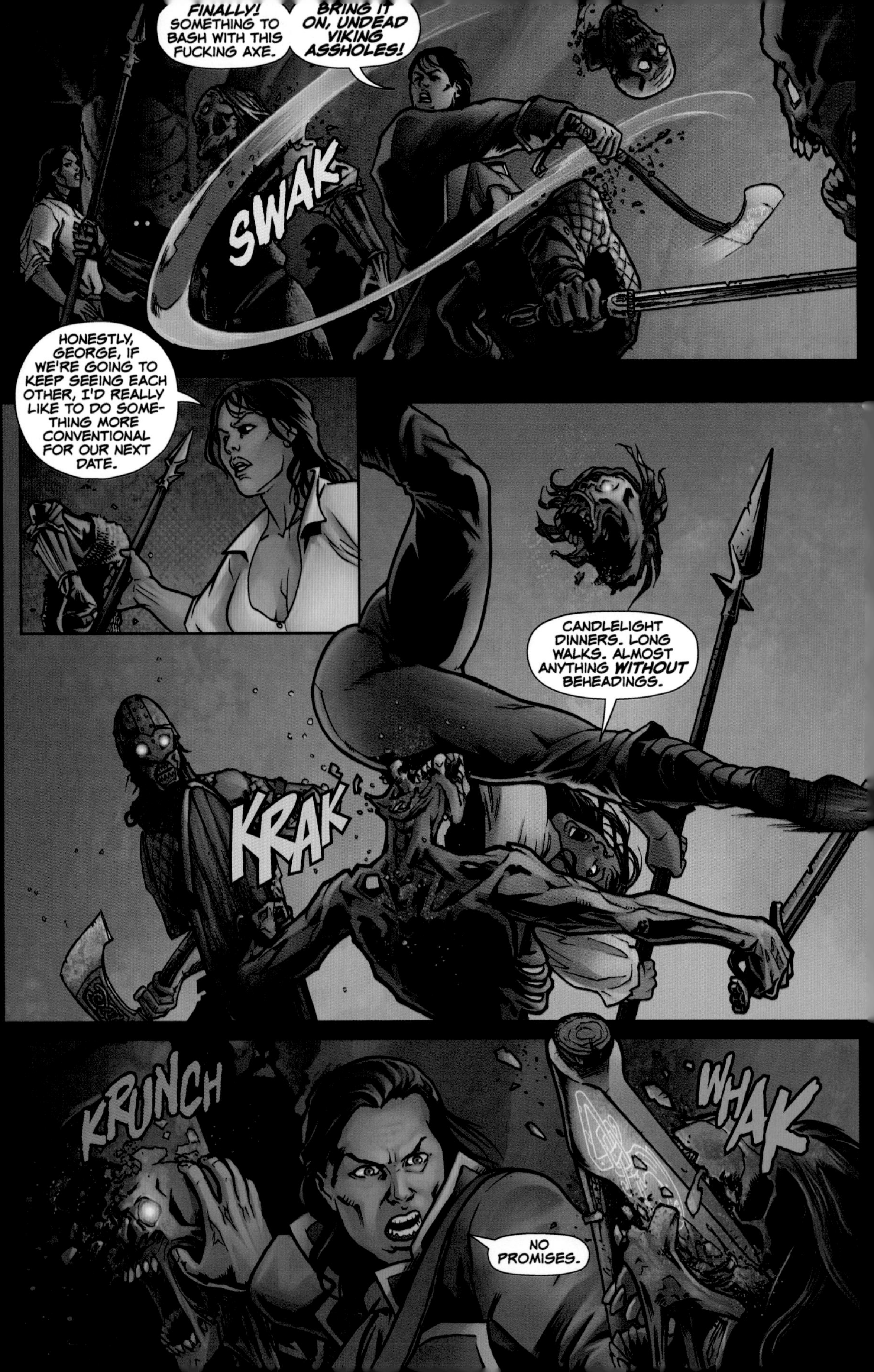
FINALLY! SOMETHING TO BASH WITH THIS FUCKING AXE.
BRING IT ON, UNDEAD VIKING ASSHOLES!
SWAK
HONESTLY, GEORGE, IF WE'RE GOING TO KEEP SEEING EACH OTHER, I'D REALLY LIKE TO DO SOME-THING MORE CONVENTIONAL FOR OUR NEXT DATE.
CANDLELIGHT DINNERS. LONG WALKS. ALMOST ANYTHING *WITHOUT* BEHEADINGS.
KRAK
KRUNCH
WHAK
NO PROMISES.

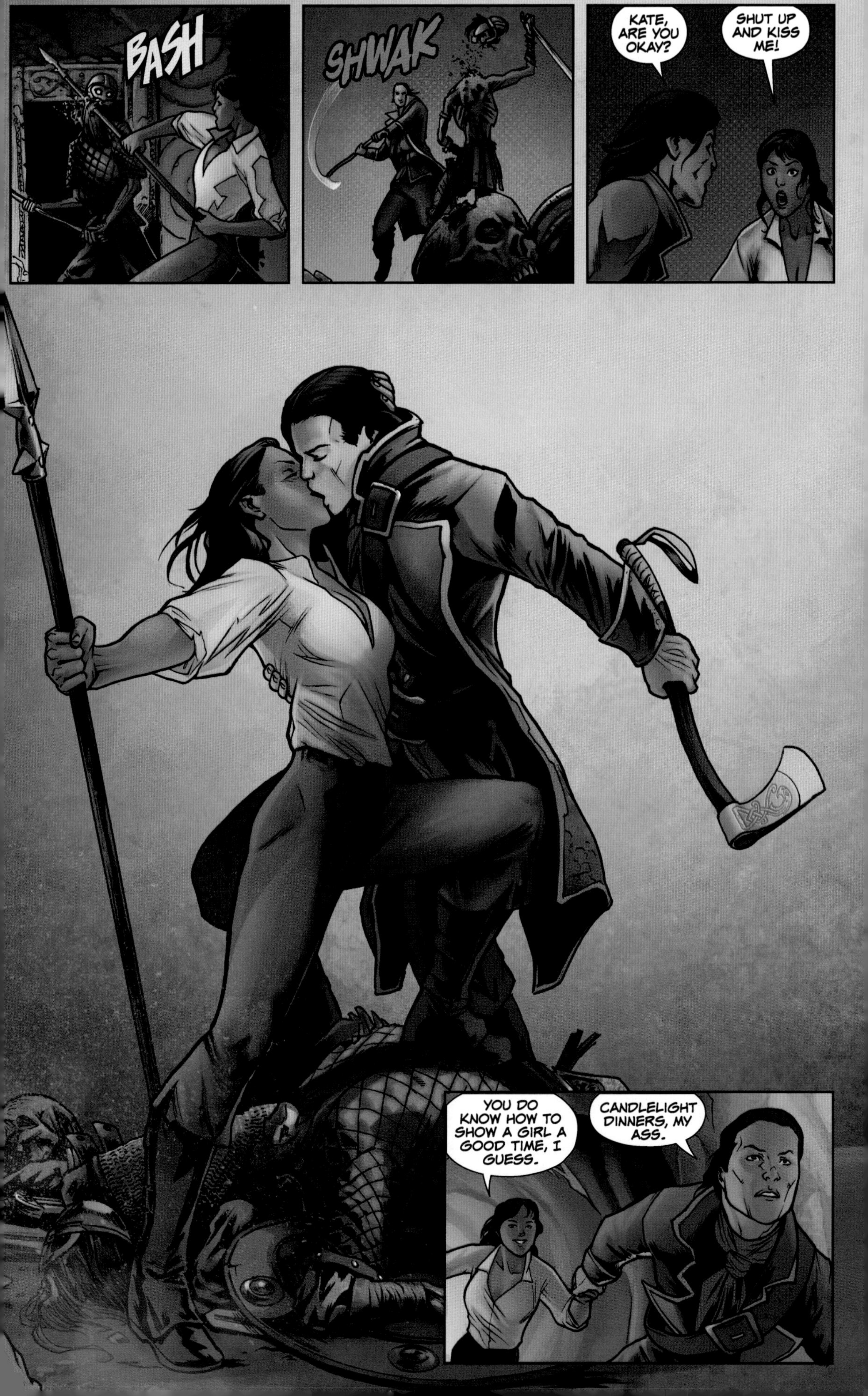
BASH
SHWAK
KATE, ARE YOU OKAY?
SHUT UP AND KISS ME!
YOU DO KNOW HOW TO SHOW A GIRL A GOOD TIME, I GUESS.
CANDLELIGHT DINNERS, MY ASS.

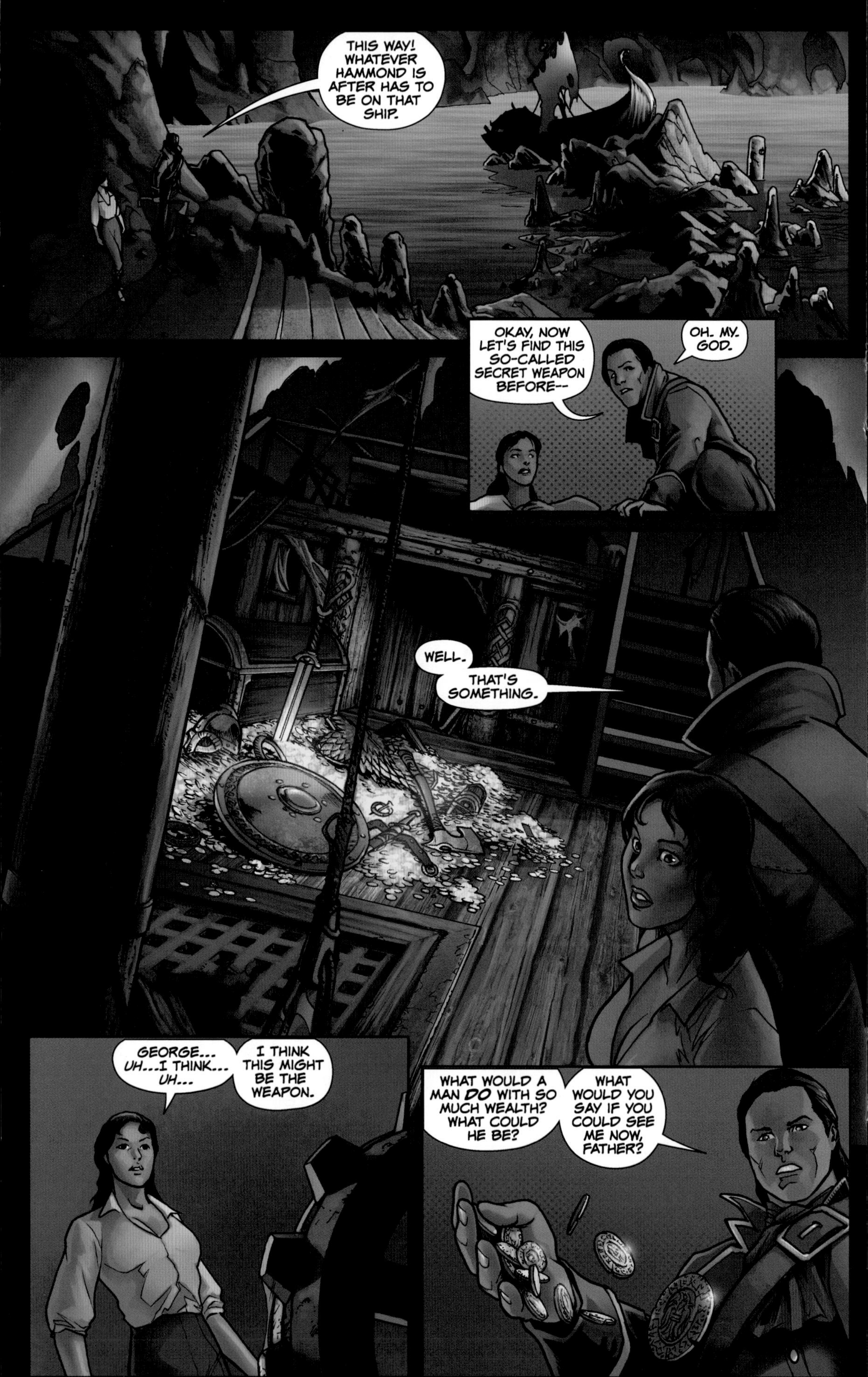
THIS WAY! WHATEVER HAMMOND IS AFTER HAS TO BE ON THAT SHIP.
OKAY, NOW LET'S FIND THIS SO-CALLED SECRET WEAPON BEFORE--
OH. MY. GOD.
WELL.
THAT'S SOMETHING.
GEORGE... UH...I THINK... UH...
I THINK THIS MIGHT BE THE WEAPON.
WHAT WOULD A MAN DO WITH SO MUCH WEALTH? WHAT COULD HE BE?
WHAT WOULD YOU SAY IF YOU COULD SEE ME NOW, FATHER?

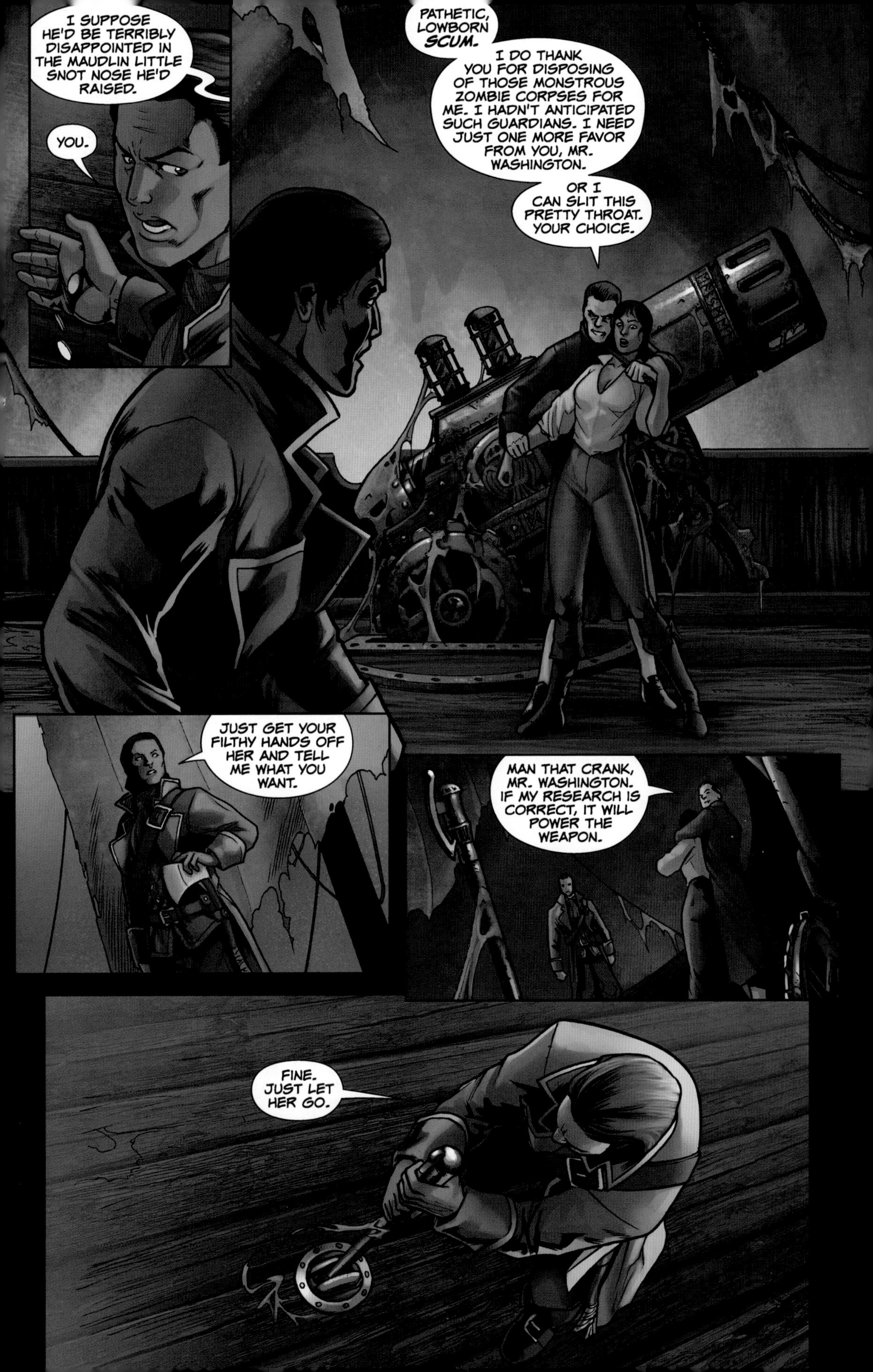
I SUPPOSE HE'D BE TERRIBLY DISAPPOINTED IN THE MAUDLIN LITTLE SNOT NOSE HE'D RAISED.
YOU.
PATHETIC, LOWBORN SCUM.
I DO THANK YOU FOR DISPOSING OF THOSE MONSTROUS ZOMBIE CORPSES FOR ME. I HADN'T ANTICIPATED SUCH GUARDIANS. I NEED JUST ONE MORE FAVOR FROM YOU, MR. WASHINGTON.
OR I CAN SLIT THIS PRETTY THROAT. YOUR CHOICE.
JUST GET YOUR FILTHY HANDS OFF HER AND TELL ME WHAT YOU WANT.
MAN THAT CRANK, MR. WASHINGTON. IF MY RESEARCH IS CORRECT, IT WILL POWER THE WEAPON.
FINE. JUST LET HER GO.

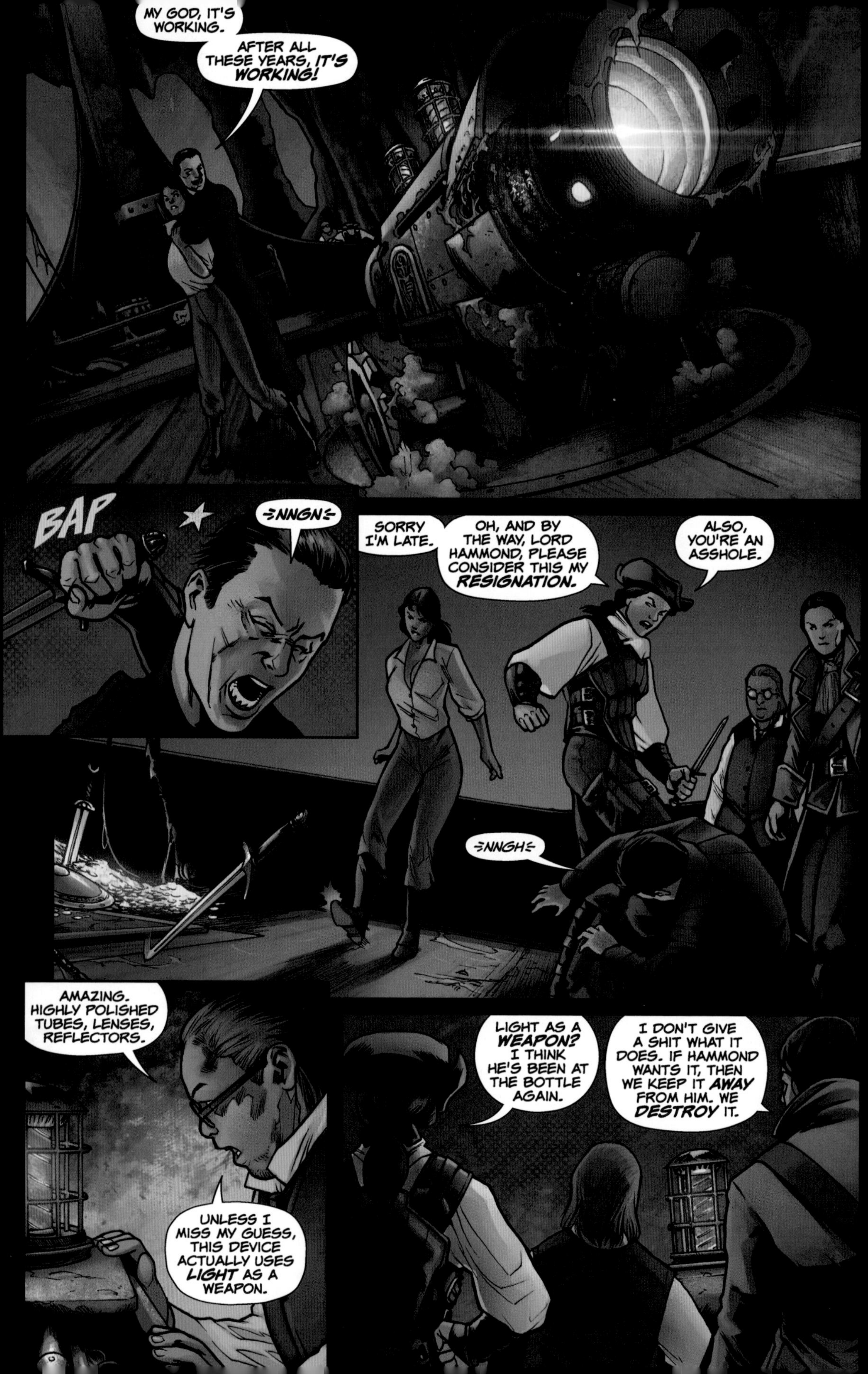
MY GOD, IT'S WORKING.
AFTER ALL THESE YEARS, IT'S WORKING!
BAP
NNGN
SORRY I'M LATE.
OH, AND BY THE WAY, LORD HAMMOND, PLEASE CONSIDER THIS MY RESIGNATION.
ALSO, YOU'RE AN ASSHOLE.
NNGH
AMAZING. HIGHLY POLISHED TUBES, LENSES, REFLECTORS.
UNLESS I MISS MY GUESS, THIS DEVICE ACTUALLY USES LIGHT AS A WEAPON.
LIGHT AS A WEAPON? I THINK HE'S BEEN AT THE BOTTLE AGAIN.
I DON'T GIVE A SHIT WHAT IT DOES. IF HAMMOND WANTS IT, THEN WE KEEP IT AWAY FROM HIM. WE DESTROY IT.

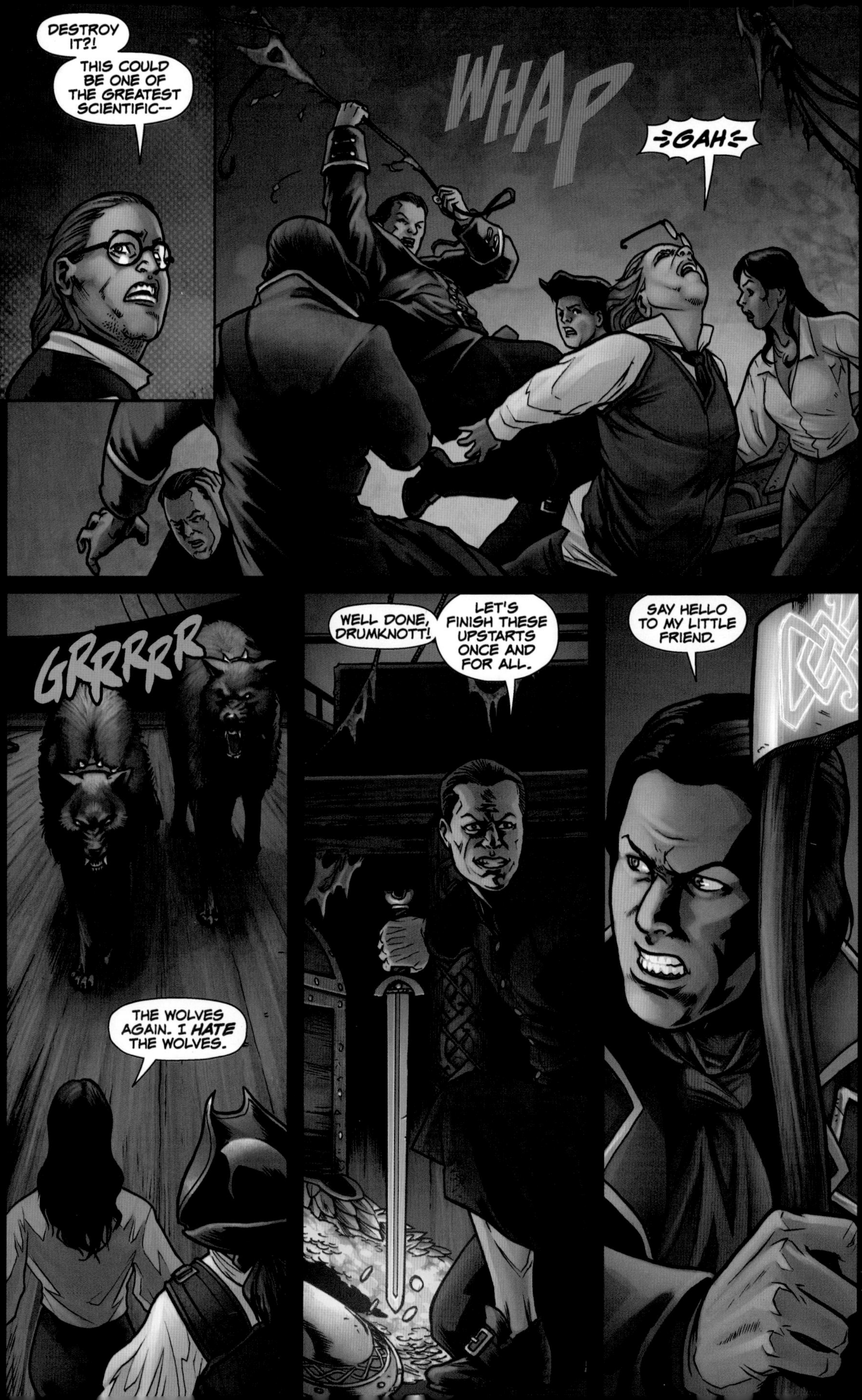
DESTROY IT?! THIS COULD BE ONE OF THE GREATEST SCIENTIFIC--
WHAP
GAH
GRRRRR
THE WOLVES AGAIN. I *HATE* THE WOLVES.
WELL DONE, DRUMKNOTT!
LET'S FINISH THESE UPSTARTS ONCE AND FOR ALL.
SAY HELLO TO MY LITTLE FRIEND.

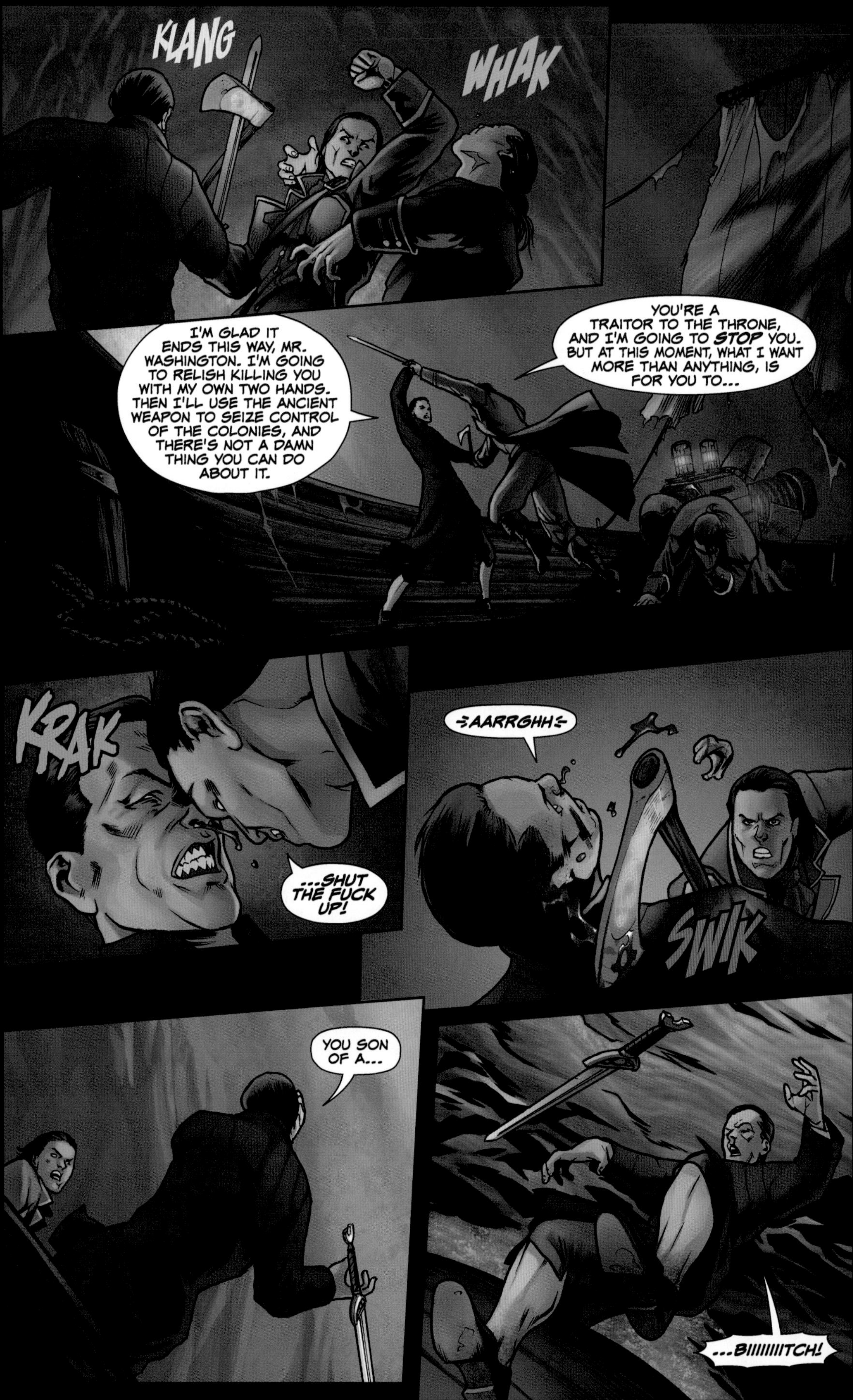
KLANG
WHAK
I'M GLAD IT ENDS THIS WAY, MR. WASHINGTON. I'M GOING TO RELISH KILLING YOU WITH MY OWN TWO HANDS. THEN I'LL USE THE ANCIENT WEAPON TO SEIZE CONTROL OF THE COLONIES, AND THERE'S NOT A DAMN THING YOU CAN DO ABOUT IT.
YOU'RE A TRAITOR TO THE THRONE, AND I'M GOING TO STOP YOU. BUT AT THIS MOMENT, WHAT I WANT MORE THAN ANYTHING, IS FOR YOU TO...
KRAK
...SHUT THE FUCK UP!
AARRGHH
SWIK
YOU SON OF A...
...BIIIIIIITCH!

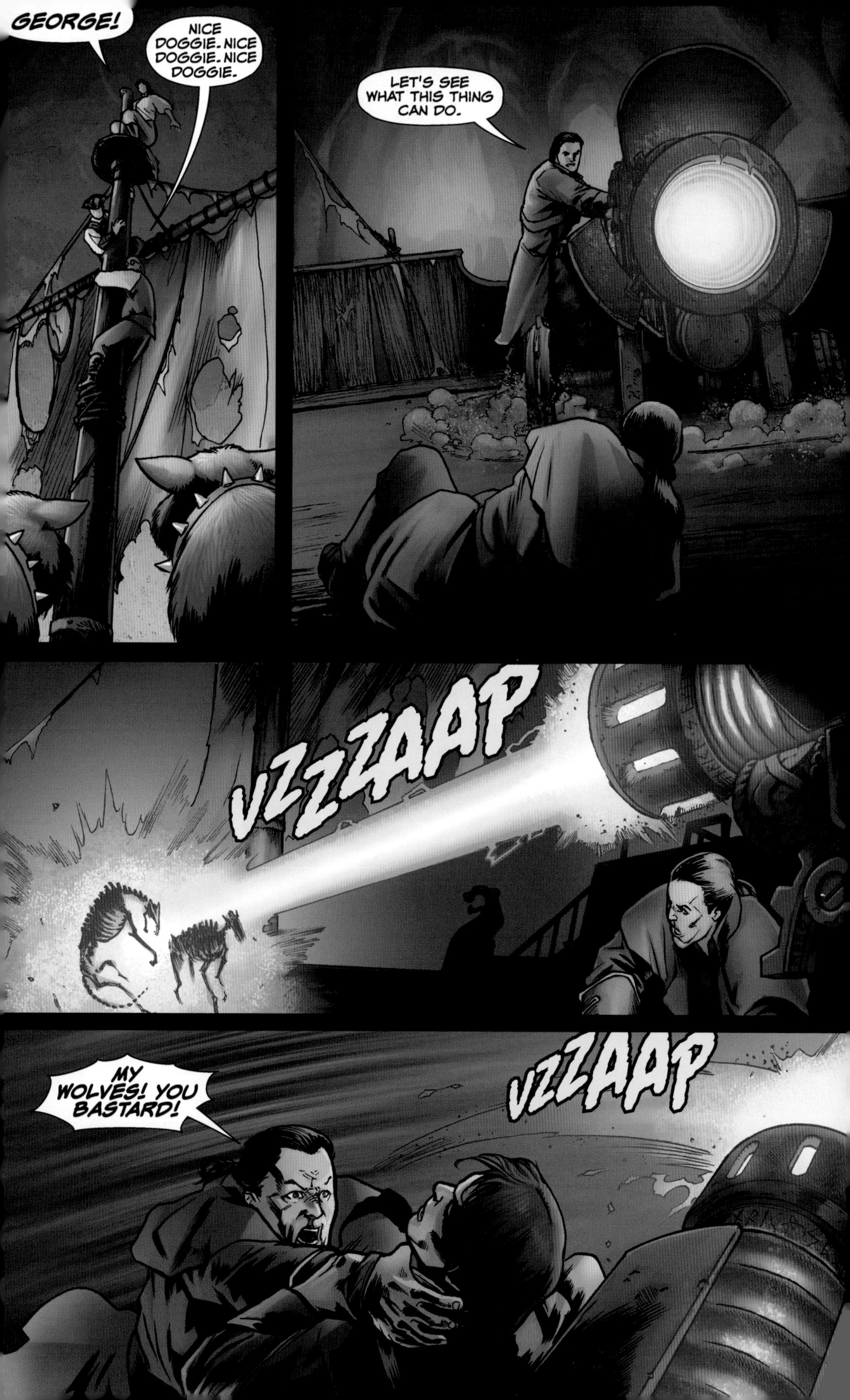
GEORGE!
NICE DOGGIE. NICE DOGGIE. NICE DOGGIE.
LET'S SEE WHAT THIS THING CAN DO.
VZZZAAP
MY WOLVES! YOU BASTARD!
VZZAAP

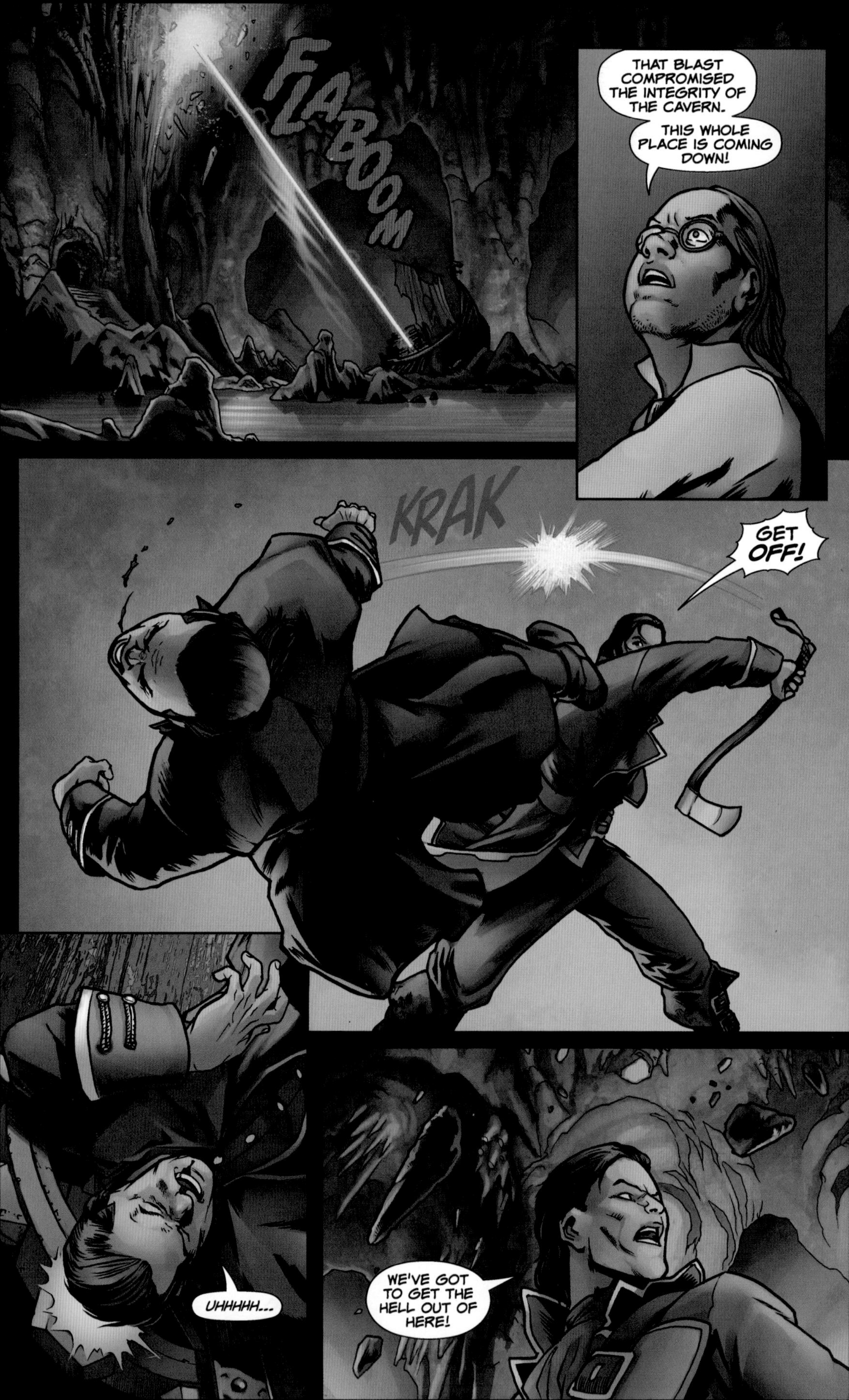
FLABOOM
THAT BLAST COMPROMISED THE INTEGRITY OF THE CAVERN.
THIS WHOLE PLACE IS COMING DOWN!
KRAK
GET OFF!
UHHHHH...
WE'VE GOT TO GET THE HELL OUT OF HERE!

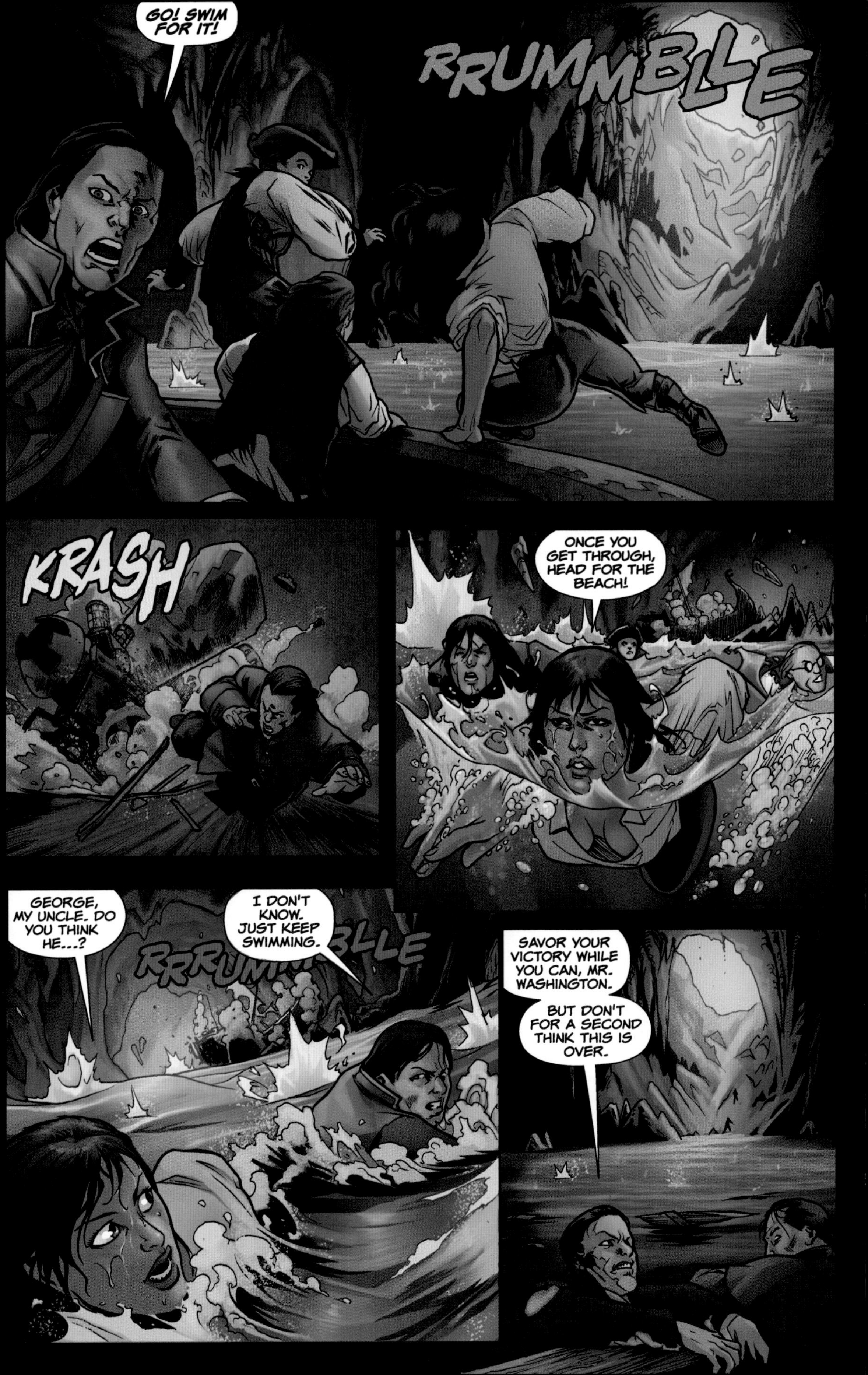
GO! SWIM FOR IT!
RRUMMBLLE
KRASH
ONCE YOU GET THROUGH, HEAD FOR THE BEACH!
GEORGE, MY UNCLE. DO YOU THINK HE...?
RRRUM...BLLE
I DON'T KNOW. JUST KEEP SWIMMING.
SAVOR YOUR VICTORY WHILE YOU CAN, MR. WASHINGTON.
BUT DON'T FOR A SECOND THINK THIS IS OVER.

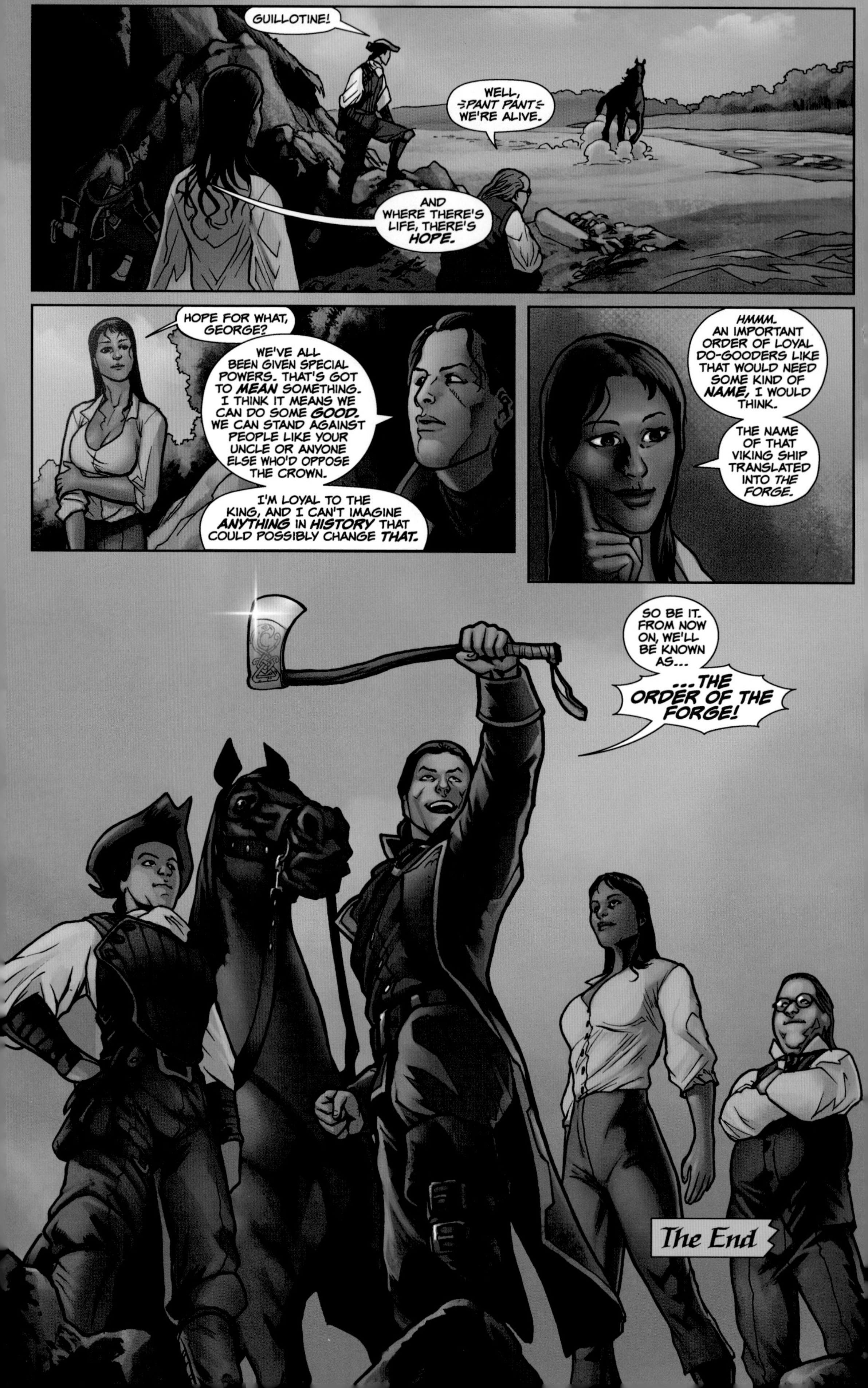
GUILLOTINE!
WELL, PANT PANT WE'RE ALIVE.
AND WHERE THERE'S LIFE, THERE'S HOPE.
HOPE FOR WHAT, GEORGE?
WE'VE ALL BEEN GIVEN SPECIAL POWERS. THAT'S GOT TO MEAN SOMETHING. I THINK IT MEANS WE CAN DO SOME GOOD. WE CAN STAND AGAINST PEOPLE LIKE YOUR UNCLE OR ANYONE ELSE WHO'D OPPOSE THE CROWN.
I'M LOYAL TO THE KING, AND I CAN'T IMAGINE ANYTHING IN HISTORY THAT COULD POSSIBLY CHANGE THAT.
HMMM. AN IMPORTANT ORDER OF LOYAL DO-GOODERS LIKE THAT WOULD NEED SOME KIND OF NAME, I WOULD THINK.
THE NAME OF THAT VIKING SHIP TRANSLATED INTO THE FORGE.
SO BE IT. FROM NOW ON, WE'LL BE KNOWN AS...
...THE ORDER OF THE FORGE!
The End

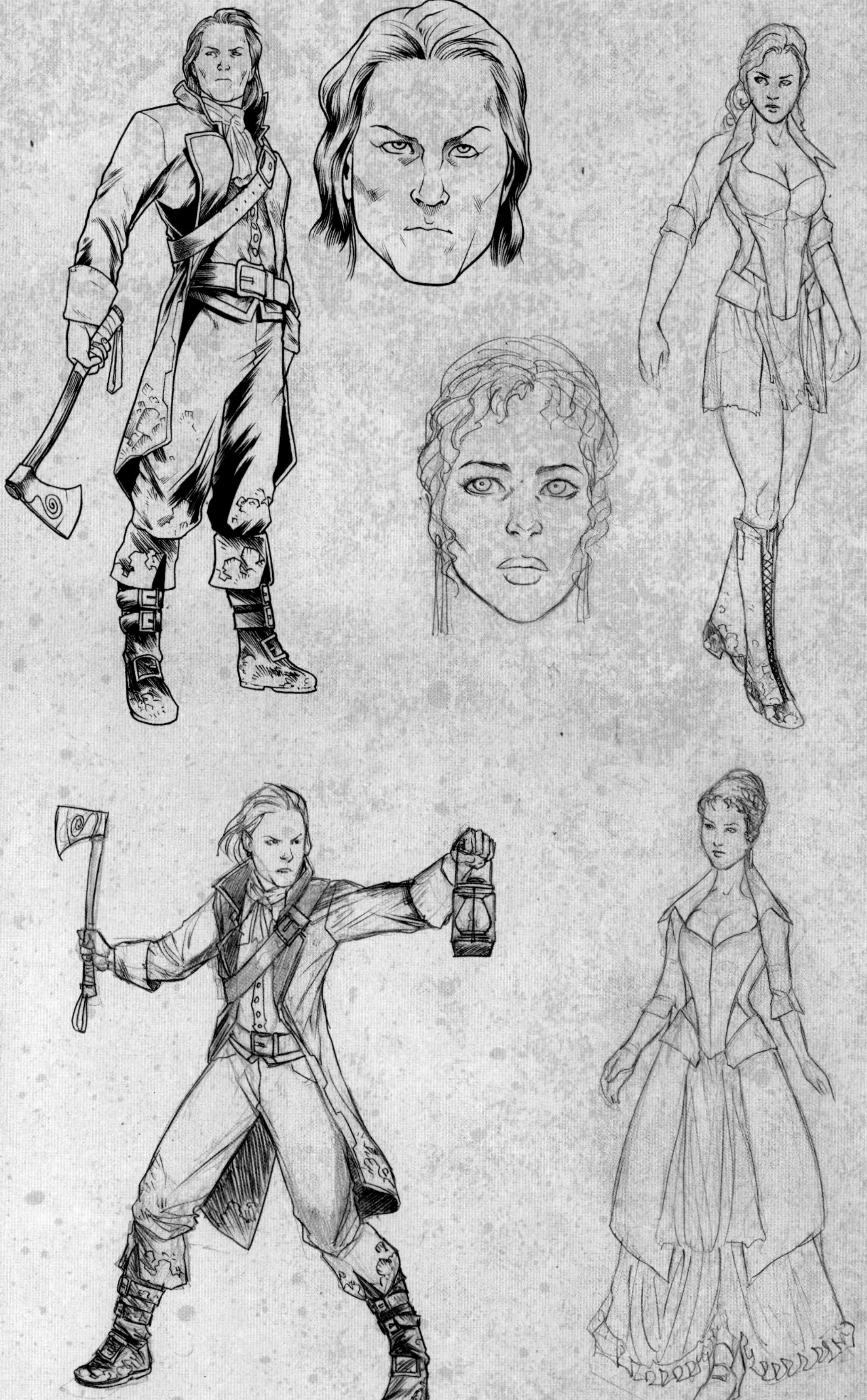

Character sketches of George Washington and Kate.

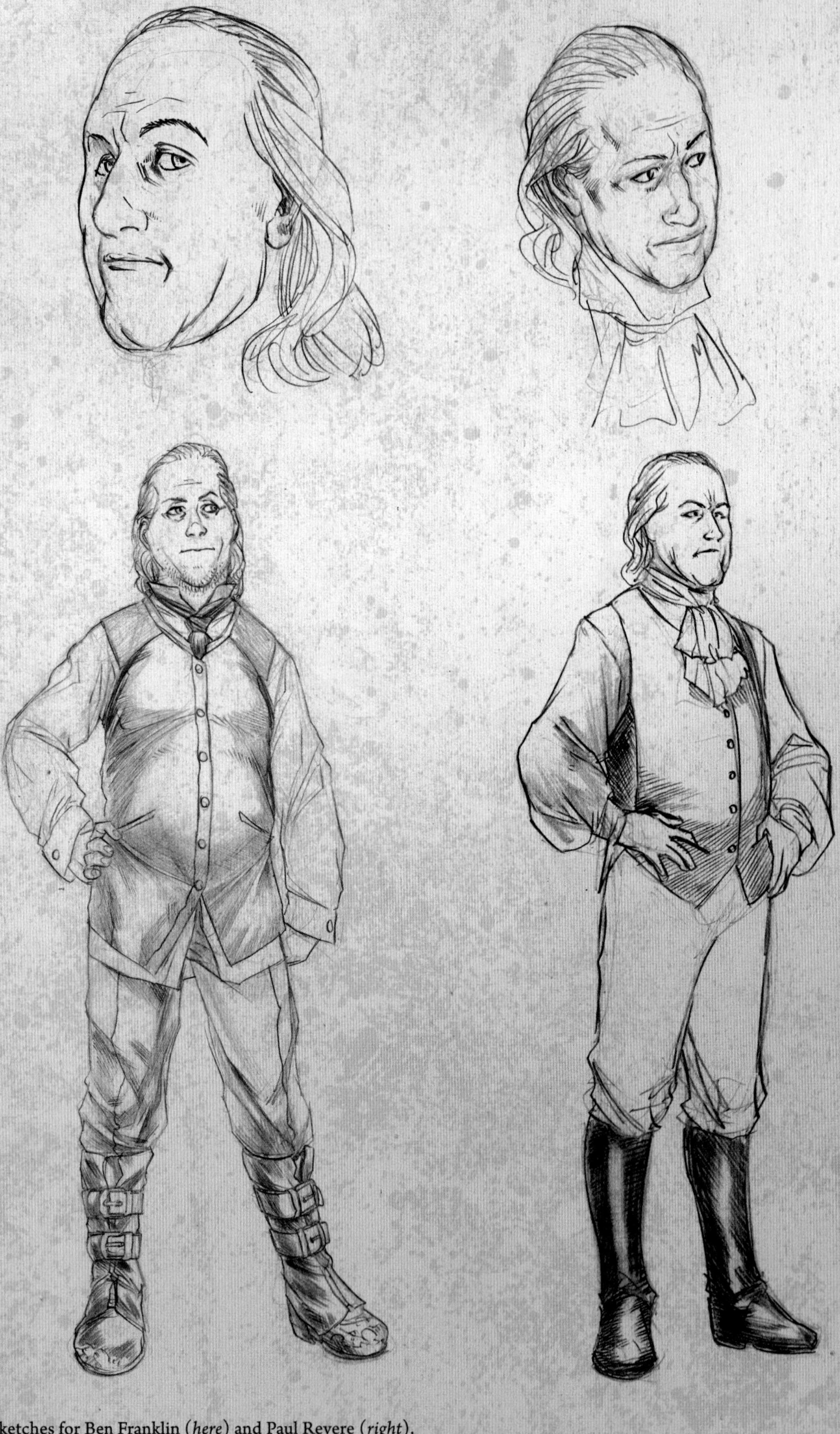

Sketches for Ben Franklin (*here*) and Paul Revere (*right*).

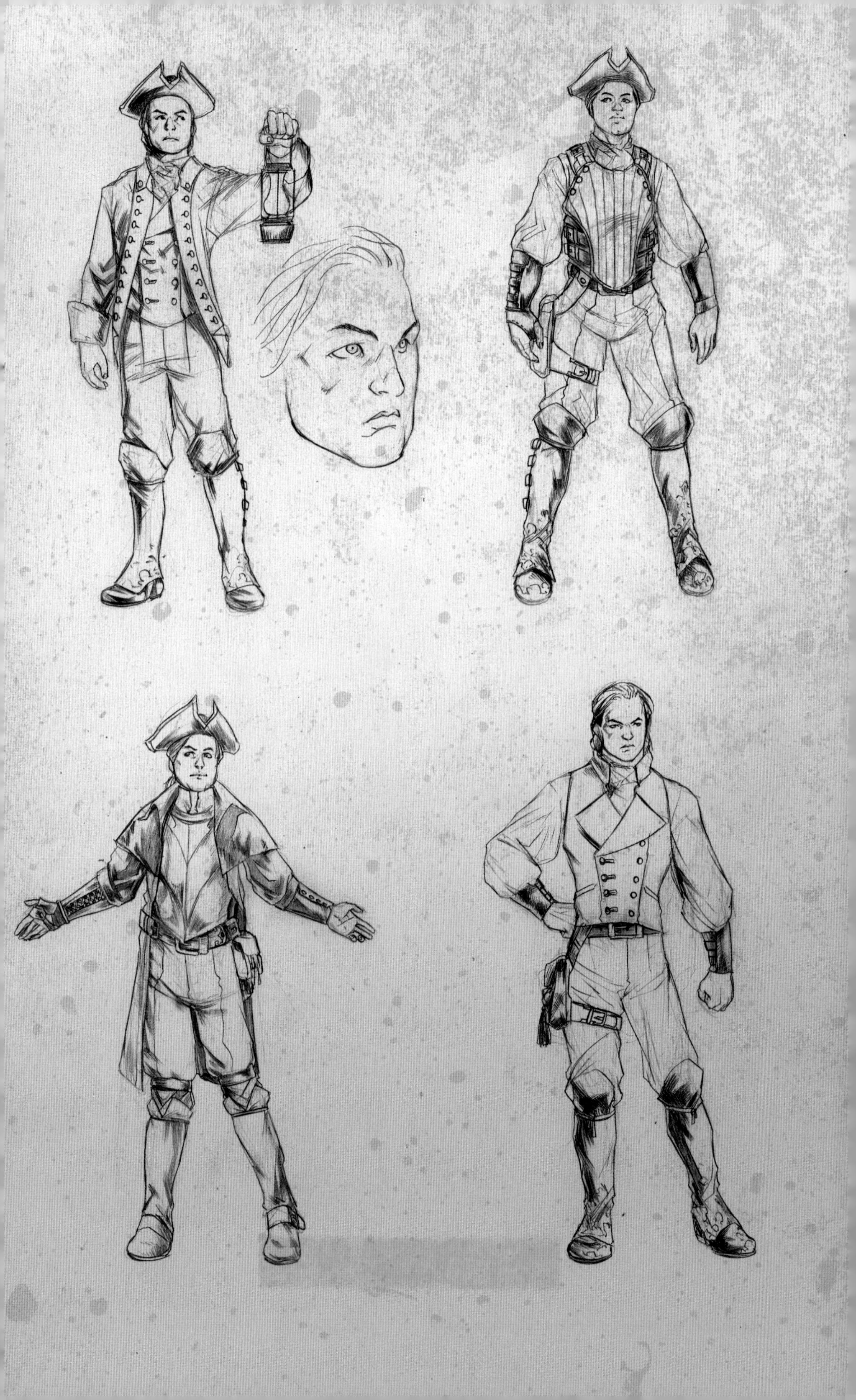

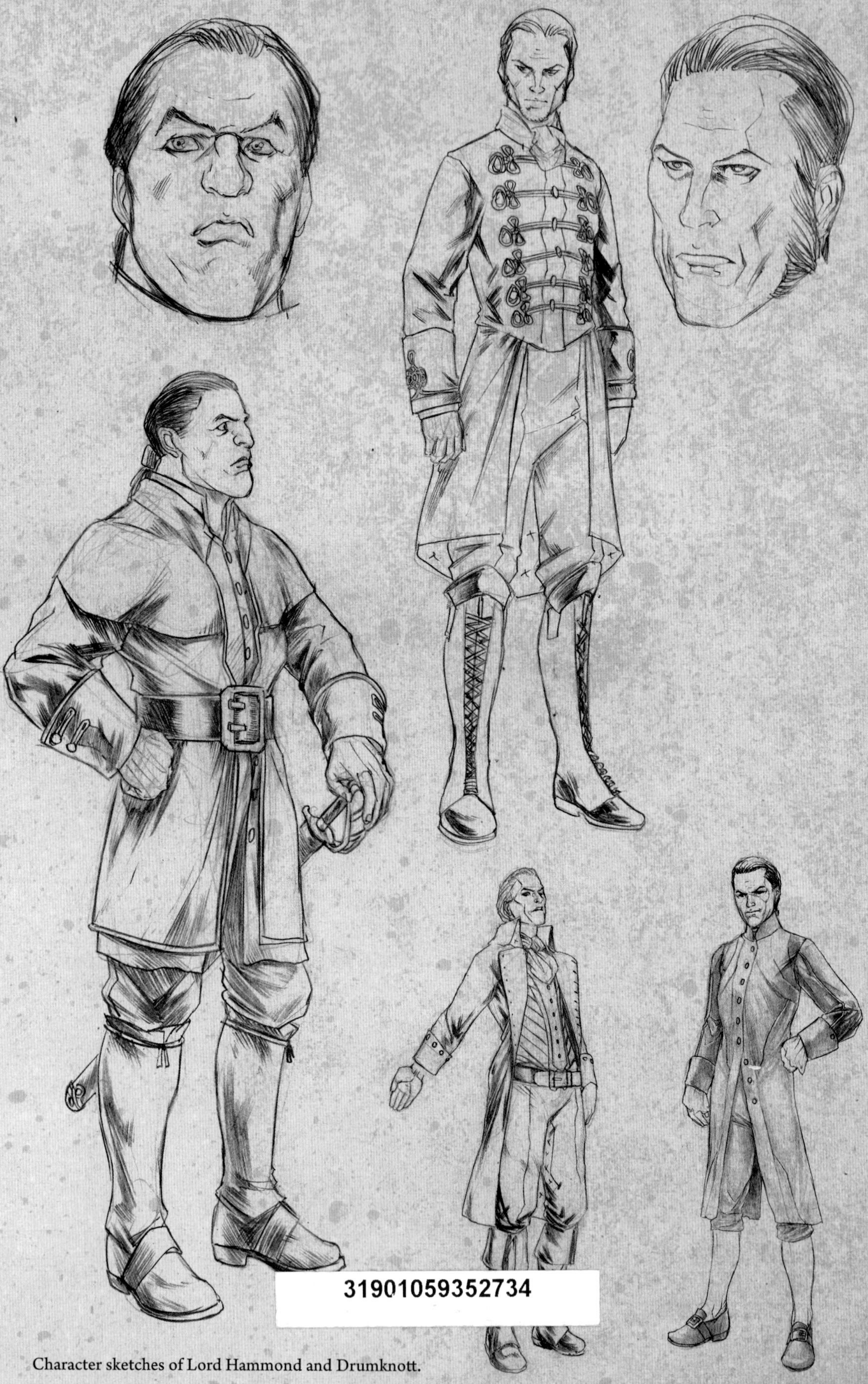

Character sketches of Lord Hammond and Drumknott.